PEACE

in your mind, heart, and soul.

SHARHONDA D. WILLIAMS

Peace, in your mind, body, and soul

Ordering Information:
Questions. Quantity sales. Special
discounts are available on quantity purchases
by corporations, associations, and others. For
details, contact the publisher at the address
above. Orders by U.S. trade bookstores and
wholesalers.

Please contact the author:
authorsharhonda@gmail.com
www.sharhondadwilliams.com

Hard Cover ISBN: 9781736171523
Paper Back ISBN: 978-1-7361715-4-7
Library of Congress: 2023923778

*Credits: Book cover, editing, and formatting
ShaRhonda D. Williams*

ShaRhonda D. Williams 2

Table Of Contents

Foreword

In our most intimate moments of prayer, we were reminded of a profound truth: true peace is found in God alone. Our journey, marked by rocky years in our marriage, was a testament to this realization. When we removed God from the center of our lives, chaos ensued, driven by fear and circumstance. However, we found solace in repentance, humbly acknowledging our transgressions, and seeking redemption. In His infinite mercy, God delivered us from the shackles of our past, graciously accepting our plea to reclaim His rightful place in our hearts and home.

With renewed dedication, we surrendered our lives anew to His divine will, inviting His sovereign presence to reign supreme once more.

In the wake of this realignment, God revealed His purpose with startling clarity: my wife was to be the vessel through which the message of peace would be shared with the world. For in our own journey, we had tasted the sweet fruits of true peace, born from our

ShaRhonda D. Williams

reconnection with the Lord. Thus, as she pens her testament to this transformative journey, she becomes a living testament to the boundless grace and abiding peace that flow from a life surrendered to God's loving embrace.

Daelon Williams

Psalm 23

A song of David.

*"The Lord is my shepherd. I will always
have everything I need.
He gives me green pastures to lie in. He
leads me by calm pools of water.
He restores my strength. He leads me on
right paths to show that he is good.
Even if I walk through a valley as dark as
the grave, I will not be afraid of any danger,
because you are with me. Your rod and staff
comfort me.
You prepared a meal for me in front of my
enemies. You welcomed me as an honored
guest. My cup is full and spilling over.
Your goodness and mercy will be with me
all my life, and I will live in the Lord's house a
long, long time."* **ICB.**

LET THE PEACE THAT CHRIST GIVES CONTROL YOUR THINKING. IT IS FOR PEACE THAT YOU WERE CHOSEN TO BE TOGETHER IN ONE BODY. AND ALWAYS BE THANKFUL.

Colossians 3:15 ERV

Introduction

This book about Peace was birthed in my prayer closet. I simply asked the Lord what my next book was about, and he said, Peace. I had a different idea of what I wanted to write my next book about, which was Depression. However, obedience to Christ triumphs my own desires. My previous book ***"How God Saved Me from The Nightmare Of Domestic Violence"*** I spoke about how I had so much turbulence in my mind. Even driving in my car alone in total silence, I experienced zero peace. I begged God to deliver me so that I could have peace and not have a racing mind. I went through hallucinations, panic attacks, and intense fear. God restored peace in my mind by praying, fasting, obeying him, and renewing my mind with his word. Being in an abusive relationship creates a sense of fight-or-flight mode. You never know what's going to happen, which makes your life feel unsafe and unpredictable. Now, you won't be able to know everything, but you don't want to fear anything except the true and living God. Once God saves you from the sin you got yourself in, don't look back and don't go back. Now, no matter what chaos or confusion may be around me, I trust in the Lord, obey the Lord, and hope in the Lord. I truly believe Psalm 91 for my life. I have seen it with my eyes. No harm came near me when it's was so close. Protection is in God's will for your life. Trust him. Obey him. Repent for your sins. Renounce your old ways and slam shut every door (sin) that you open to give the enemy legal right to attack you. If you disobey God and do not repent, you open the door for the evil one to come, make himself a home in you. Be warned that the scriptures say the enemy is literally lurking around looking for who he can kill, steal from, and ultimately destroy. What does he want to kill? Your relationship with God. He wants to kill your spirit, man. He wants to kill your passions. He wants to kill your desire to renew your mind with the word of God. He wants to steal your peace, hope, your destiny, and your inheritance from God. He wants to destroy anything good. Your marriage, your children, your relationships, your family, your Godly friendships, your church, your name, and your blessings.

ShaRhonda D. Williams

Here in this book, you will learn the difference between peace and quiet, the fruits of the spirit painted into pictures for your mind, Greek translations of the word, and where to find them in scripture. You will learn fruits of the flesh and just how deadly they are to indulge in. You will leave being clear on how God wants us to live this Christian life. If you know these things, you will be able to live a life for Christ that is peaceful because you walk in the fruits of the spirit instead of the fruits of the flesh (sin). Sin will open the door and consume your peace like a fire. But if you walk in the spirit, you will hold on to your peace despite any fiery dart the enemy throws at you. You will find yourself blameless because you live a life of repentance and devotion to your Lord and Savior, Jesus Christ. My prayer is that you read this book in its entirety and utilize the resources. May any blinders on your eyes be removed, may any plugs over your ears be taken out, may you be able to truly see God's desires for you in your walk with Christ through this book. May your love and relationship with Christ be stronger. May you be on fire for God and bold in sharing his gospel with the people. May you stand up for truth and chase righteousness even when it's popular to stand for lies and lawlessness. May you be delivered from any chains of sin that have you bound. May you be obedient to God's original design for our lives despite your feelings. May the word of God (holy bible) be your final authority in Jesus name AMEN.

ShaRhonda D. Williams 11

Salvation

First things first let's get you saved. The Lord told me to offer salvation first in this book. So, in obedience to him here is the offer.

If you desire to be saved, *"this is what the Scripture says: "God's teaching is near you; it is in your mouth and in your heart." It is the teaching of faith that we tell people. If you openly say, "Jesus is Lord" and believe in your heart that God raised him from death, you will be saved. Yes, we believe in Jesus deep in our hearts, and so we are made right with God. And we openly say that we believe in him, and so we are saved. Yes, the Scriptures say, "Anyone who trusts in him will never be disappointed."* **Romans 10: 8-11**Repeat this prayer: Father in the name of Jesus thank you for dying on the cross for my sins, father forgive me for all my sins, come into my heart and give me a clean heart and a right spirit. Cleanse me from all unrighteousness help me to know you and to love you. Reveal yourself to me in a way that I know for certain it is you. Deliver my soul and set me free from the evil one. I accept you Jesus as my Lord and savior and give you full range to rule, reign, dwell, and abide in my heart. Holy Spirit have your way. Lord let your will be done here on earth in my life as it is in heaven in Jesus name AMEN.

Lord, I thank you for this new believer's life. I pray Lord that you have mercy on them, forgive them their sin, and completely deliver them from all unrighteousness. Lord, I pray just like a newborn baby that you cover them and hide them from the enemy in plain sight. Lord, I pray that all the nurture, love, maturing, resources, revelations, and understanding that they need come to them in the mighty name of Jesus. Lord shows them how much you truly love them in Jesus name.

Rededication back to God

God has been telling me over and over the time to get right with God is now! If you have already accepted Jesus as your Lord and savior but you feel far from God and disconnected. This is my plea and call for you to REPENT and return to your first love. Prodigal son and prodigal daughter return home now, for the kingdom of God is near!!! It doesn't matter what you've done and where you've been. Just surrender your will and return to the father. Humble yourself and pray before it's too late so that God can hear you from heaven and forgive your sins and heal your land. Being in right standing with God is more important than the guilt and shame that Satan is trying to make you carry. Confess your sins to God and ask him to forgive you. Renounce those things you did.

ShaRhonda D. Williams 14

Come out of agreement with them now. Break covenant with them now. Denounce them now. Repent now. ABANDON those sins you loved so much. If you don't, they shall surely be the death of you. Just like they rejoice when the prodigal son returned, so will we when you repent. Just like he left the 99 for the 1 lost sheep, surely will we rejoice over you when you return and repent. The kingdom of God needs you, and it is better with you. Come home, brothers and sisters! You are welcomed here!

I pray that every lost sheep reading this writing is restored back to the father. I pray that the veil is lifted off your eyes, and that God has mercy on you. I pray that God shows you he still loves you and you can repent and get back in right standing with him. I pray that you confess everything you did. I pray that you renounce pride and come into covenant with humility. I pray that you will seek God's face by crying out to him on your face and accepting Jesus back into your heart as your Lord and Savior to rule, reign, dwell, and abide in you! I pray that everything the enemy stole from you is returned. Every dream, destiny, birthrights, and blessing that were stolen from you will be restored to you, the rightful owner. I pray you

ShaRhonda D. Williams 15

come back into your right mind. I pray that every mind control spirit is loosed off you. I pray you snap out of the trance that you are in. I come against any spells that you are on. I plead the blood of Jesus over your mind and life. I pray God sends his angels to surround you and protect you. I pray God directs and leads your paths back to right standing with him in the mighty name of Jesus.

Make personal your desire to rededicate your life to God, your confessions (tell him everything), asking for forgiveness, forgiving others, and be ye reconciled back to your first love in the mighty name of Jesus.

If you have already accepted Jesus as your Lord and savior but you feel far from God and disconnected. This is my plea and call for you to REPENT and return to your first love. Prodigal son and prodigal daughter return home now for the kingdom of God is near!!! It doesn't matter what you've done and where you've been. Just surrender your will and return to the father. Humble yourself and pray before it's too late so that God can hear you from heaven and forgive your sins and heal your land. Being in right standing with God is more important than the guilt and shame that Satan is trying to make you carry. Confess your sins to God and ask him to forgive you. Renounce those things you did. Come out of agreement with them now. Break covenant with them now. Denounce them now. Repent now. ABANDON those sins you loved so much. If you don't, they shall surely be the death of you. Just like they rejoice when the prodigal son returned so will we when you repent. Just like he left the 99 for the 1 lost sheep surely will we rejoice over you when you return and repent. The kingdom of God needs you and it is better with you. Come home brothers and sisters! You are welcomed here!

I pray that every lost sheep reading this writing is restored back to the father. I pray that the veil is lifted off your eyes and that God has mercy on you. I pray that God shows you he still loves you and you can repent and get back in right standing with him. I pray that you confess everything you did. I pray that you renounce pride and come into covenant with humility. I pray that you will seek God's face by crying out to him on your face and accepting Jesus back into your heart as your Lord and Savior to rule, reign, dwell, and abide in you! I pray that everything the enemy stole from you is returned. Every dream, destiny, birth rights, and blessing that were stolen from you will be restored to you the rightful owner. I pray that you come back into your right mind. I pray that every mind control spirit is loosed off you. I pray that you snap out of the trans that you are in. I come against any spells done on you. We tear down every wicked altar that was made to destroy you. I plead the blood of Jesus over your mind and life. I pray that God sends his angels to surround you and protect you. I pray that God directs and leads your paths back to right standing with him in the mighty name of Jesus.

Make personal your desire to rededicate your life to God, your confessions (tell him everything), asking for forgiveness, forgiving others, and be ye reconciled back to your first love in the mighty name of Jesus.

ShaRhonda D. Williams 18

Chapter 1
Peace and Quiet

    The difference between peace and quiet is simple. Quietness means there is no outside noise. Peace, on the other hand, means there is no worry inside your mind. You might experience quietness when there is no sound around you, but if your mind is racing and filled with fear, then you do not have true peace. What you might have is just a false sense of peace.

    True peace can exist even in noisy or chaotic environments. It's about having a calm and still inner state because of your trust and hope in the Lord. When you trust in God, you can let go of worries. Without worry, you can trust God through life's challenges. This is the peace that surpasses all understanding and isn't dependent on your circumstances.

Peace comes from God alone. The Bible tells us that even a mustard seed of faith can move mountains. You don't achieve peace by making everyone around you silent; instead, you find peace by asking God to calm your own thoughts. Sometimes, this might mean fasting—skipping meals to focus on prayer and reading the Bible. Peace is not just about avoiding people who have hurt you; it also means forgiving them to avoid bitterness. Let go of past wrongs and break any mental and emotional ties to them. This will help heal your heart and renew your mind.

Peace is about being free from disturbances and feeling calm inside. So, even if it's quiet around you, if your mind is still troubled, you don't have peace. Watch your thoughts over the next few days to see if your mind is truly at peace. If you're fixated on revenge or holding grudges, you are not at peace; your mind is in conflict. This mental turmoil can tire you out, even if you haven't done anything physically.

Some people find it hard to be alone with their thoughts because they bring fear, shame, and regret. Instead of letting these thoughts control you. Learn to speak God's word against those thoughts. Just like in 1 Corinthians 10:5 ERV "And we tear down every proud idea that raises itself against the knowledge of God. We also capture every thought and make it give up and obey Christ." What's a proud idea? Any thought that is against God's word. Proud means it thinks it knows better than God's word. Any thought that makes you rebel against God, rebel against God's word, against God's order, against the way God designed. Another example can be that your ex doesn't deserve your forgiveness because what they did to you was evil. That is a proud thought because the Bible says we must forgive or we won't be forgiven. If you have experienced trauma, like abuse or betrayal, address these issues by asking God to heal you, confess to him how you truly feel, repenting for your own mistakes, forgiving those who wrong you, forgiving yourself, breaking harmful agreements, and seeking God's healing. Taking accountability for yourself, your thoughts, and actions will have you reevaluate your decisions.

Remember, those who have hurt you don't have to control your life. Forgiveness unlocks the control they have over you. You can move past overthinking and find freedom from mental anguish. Quietness is simply no outside noise, but peace is found in the state of your own mind. We can't read others' thoughts, but we can evaluate our own. If you struggle with this, I've included a prayer at the end of the book to help you find inner peace.

In the upcoming chapters, we will explore the fruits of the Spirit as described in the Bible, and how these qualities guide us in our daily lives. This book is written in a everyday tone to make these concepts easier to understand. We will also discuss the fruits of the flesh and how they can impact your peace. My prayer is as you learn that you grow, mature, and make decisions that will increase you peace.

As you read, I encourage you to reflect on whether you are exhibiting any of the fruits of the flesh and consider how this might be affecting your peace. It's important to recognize that once you understand, through the Bible, what behaviors are wrong, you have the responsibility to make a choice.

Remember, you can always confess your shortcomings to God, repent, and seek His forgiveness. It is only too late when you have passed away. The Bible says, "My people are destroyed for lack of knowledge" (Hosea 4:6 KJV). May this knowledge open your eyes, lead you to humility, and inspire you to pray and repent.

There is no need to punish yourself for past mistakes. God loves you and is just to forgive you. Now, with the understanding and knowledge you have gained, it is time to make informed choices. This book is dedicated to both new believers and those who may have strayed from their faith.

> " Father, in the name of Jesus I pray that you still my mind. I command every demon that has followed me, was sent to me, or transferred to me to leave me now in Jesus name. I pray that you lift every heavy dark cloud from me, every burden, worry, and concern. Lord teach me how to be at peace. Lord help me to be in a sound mind and sound heart in Jesus name. Help me not to have a mind that over works, that is anxious, and fearful. Help me to trust in you Lord and submit to your perfect will in my life. Help me not confuse quietness with peace but give me a true understanding of the importance and difference between the two.
> In Jesus Name AMEN. "

ShaRhonda D. Williams 24

Word Of The Lord

The Lord told me to encourage you with Jeremiah 29:11 ERV "I have good plans for you. I don't plan to hurt you. I plan to give you hope and a good future." He said to remind them he hears the prayers of the righteous. We are called to be holy women and men of valor (great courage in the face of danger). The time to get right with God is NOW! You are loved. You are blood brought, and you are commanded to honor God with your life. You will not get ahead in life operating in the fruits of the flesh. It may seem like you are, but you're only excelling to destruction. The top is not what people think it is. It really is the bottom. The ones who believe God, fear God, honor God, and pick up their cross daily to follow God, obey him, and renew their mind with his word are at the top. The ones who take heed of the holy spirit's instructions.

ShaRhonda D. Williams 25

He sent the holy spirit as a helper according to his word. Stop ignoring him. Your own way is leading you to hell not only eternally, but in your life now. I see the tears you cry at night. Your spirit man longs for me, but you don't spend time with me ever. You pretend to know and love me on the internet and at church. But I never hear from you in prayer. When I warn you, you cast it down as if a good a father wouldn't warn their child whom they love about danger.

The daddy-less community has made ya'll numb. But in my word, it says I am a father to the fatherless. I am close to the brokenhearted. Why don't you believe my word? God is saying what you are missing is me. No one can get to me except through my son, Jesus. For it is his name, we send prayers up! That's how I ordained it. I don't need your permission. You are loved. You are valued. You are needed. Don't give up. I am the bread of life. I am the truth and the life. This well if you drink from it, it'll never run dry.

God said in your book, tell them it is me they are seeking. I am the void they are trying to fill. Nothing will fill that void except me. It is safety in me. Abide in me and I will abide in you. Renew your mind with my word. Examine yourselves and when horrible things you did come to mind, just repent, come out of agreement, break covenant, renounce, and denounce those things you did. Don't dwell on them. Let them go. For I have forgiven your sins as far as the north is from the south. Let it go! It's like staying in handcuffs when they let you out scotch free even though you're guilty and you were wrong. You are forgiven. Nothing is too horrible. REPENT now because after death will be too late. None know the day or time when they'll go back to dust. Every day is too long to wait to repent and get right with God. People are dropping right and left like flies, and you could always be next. REPENT for the kingdom of God is near. If you think it's so far off and you got time, you will never repent and die in your sins. REPENT, my dear child, daily.

Let go of unforgiveness that's why you have no peace. You hate everybody and you're mad at everybody else. This is paralyzing you to the point of incapacitation (deprived of strength or power). You are not growing, maturing, or changing because you have guilt and too much weight of unforgiveness, holding you down like a nail bolted to the floor. The time to forgive is NOW! Let it GO! If you do not forgive hear the

Peace, in your mind, body, and soul*

Word of the Lord, you will NOT BE FORGIVEN!
I plead with you. Forgive my child FORGIVE!

It is imperative that you spend time with me to get instructions for your life. It is not only the Pastors/Prophets/Prophetess job to come to me for instructions for you. But it is everyone's job to come to me themselves to have your own relationship with me. Your sister cannot have a relationship with your mother for you. In the same way, think of me. Come get bread for yourself. I love you just as well as my prophets, teachers, and apostles. The day is near where deception is at an all-time high. My people need to heed my voice lest ye be led astray.

ShaRhonda D. Williams 28

> So, I tell you, live the way the Spirit leads you. Then you will not do the evil things your sinful self wants. The sinful self wants what is against the Spirit, and the Spirit wants what is against the sinful self. They are always fighting against each other, so that you don't do what you really want to do. But if you let the Spirit lead you, you are not under law.
> **Galatians 5:16-18 ERV**

Chapter 2

Love

"Love covers a multitude of sins."

1 Peter 7:8 AMP

Biblical Definition of Love

In the Bible, love is more than just a feeling; it's about how we act and treat others.

Here are the key points:

1. Agape Love
   – Agape is the Bible's highest form of love. It's unconditional and selfless. This kind of love means putting others' needs before your own and not expecting anything in return. It's the

love God has for us and what He wants us to show to others.

Scripture: "God is love" (1 John 4:8) and "For

God so loved the world that he gave his one and only Son"(John 3:16).

   2. Love as a Commandment
     - The Bible teaches that love is the most important commandment. Jesus said that loving God with all your heart and loving your neighbor as yourself are the greatest commandments.

Scripture: "Love the Lord your God with all your heart and with all your soul and with all your mind... Love your neighbor as yourself" (Matthew 22:37-39).

   3. Love in Action
     - Love isn't just about words or feelings; it's about what you do. In 1 Corinthians 13, love is described as being patient, kind, and not keeping track of wrongs. It's about showing kindness and being there for others.

Scripture: "Love is patient, love is kind... It does not dishonor others, it is not self-seeking" (1 Corinthians 13:4-7).

4. Love as a Fruit of the Spirit
   - Love is listed as the first fruit of the Spirit in Galatians. This means that when we live guided by the Holy Spirit, love naturally flows from us.

Scripture: "The fruit of the Spirit is love, joy, peace..." (Galatians 5:22-23).

5. Love as Sacrificial
   - True love often involves sacrifice. Jesus showed the ultimate example of love by giving His life for us.
   Scripture: "Greater love has no one than this: to lay down one's life for one's friends." (John 15:13).

In summary, the biblical view of love is about acting selflessly, following God's commands, and showing kindness through our actions. It's not just about how we feel but how we live out that love every day.

When you love someone and they have not betrayed you, you feel strong and secure.

So, when you love them, and they betray you, it leaves you feeling heartbroken. Love is a necessity because it covers a multitude of sins.

Do you know you can feel that love from someone who'd never betray you, leave you, nor forsake you?

Picture This:

A man has a wife who, when he goes to sleep, she goes out to the bar, slips drugs into men's drinks, seduces him, takes him to a motel, has sex with him, and steals all his money and jewelry. The wife does this night after night for years. Then one day the husband says to the wife I love you, come back to me. You don't have to do this. The wife says but I want to. Then the husband says okay. I love you. I'm always here if you need me. Then goes to sleep. Wife leaves out to prowl. One night, her husband secretly follows her. He watches from afar. He notices that the man she plans to seduce switches the drink and his wife ends up with the drugged drink, but she doesn't drink it. She leaves with the victim and her husband follows them. They get to the motel. The husband watches them go into the room. The wife sleeps with the man. When she thinks her victim is asleep, she takes his money and jewelry and rushes out the door. As she opens the door, her husband is at the door. He says, baby, please come home! He's weeping and pleading with her. She says move. I am coming home. Let's go. Shhh. They rushed to the car and all of a sudden the victim shoots and hit the husband in the back and kills him instantly. The man knew his wife was a cheater, a liar, a thief, and prostituting herself for money. Yet he still loved her and came to save her and ultimately lost his life to save hers.

I wonder how this love story made you feel.

Imagine how God feels. We are God's bride. But we whore after other false gods, like money, power, sex, respect, pride, and all kinds of selfish ambitions.

Remember, I asked if you knew someone who would love you, who would never betray you, leave you, or forsake you? That someone is Jesus. In the scriptures it tells us how God loved the world so much he sent his one and only son Jesus to be the sacrifice for our sins. God said he is married to the backslidder and to come back to him. Return, rebellious children (backslidders), declares the Lord, for I'm your husband (married to you). I'll gather you. (I'll choose you)." Jeremiah 3:14 CEB A backslider is one who knew the Lord and loved him but left to go back to a life of sin. The Lord saying I am married means his is committed to us and in covenant with us which is a binding agreement between us and him. We are adopted into his family when we accept Jesus as our Lord and Savior. We are now considered children of God.

So, Jesus came down and performed many signs, wonders, and miracles on the earth. Ultimately, he was sacrificed on the cross for the sins of man. Even though Jesus was innocent of all charges, but he died so today you could be free and forgiven. He wanted every sin you commit to be forgiven. Therefore, he gives us the ability to repent and turn from our wicked ways. We need to renounce those sins we committed daily. And stay away from doing what God deems as evil. That's why each day as believers we need to do an inventory of what is in our heart. If you are not spending time with God daily, start today! Read his word, repent for your sins, renounce those sins, thank him, allow him to speak to you, pray in the spirit, and worship him.

Love is the first fruit of the spirit found in Galatians 5:22-23.

What is love to you? Love, in my own words, is an action word. Love is shown by how you treat a person, what you do for a person, and what you feel for them in your heart. If you love a person, you respect them. If you love a person, you support them. If you love a person, you don't hold grudges against them, instead you forgive them quickly. If you love a person, you want to see them, be successful in life. If you love a person you tell them the truth.

What does the bible say love is? This is my command: Love each other as I have loved you. *"The greatest love a person can show is to die for his friends. You are my friends if you do what I command. John 15:13-14 NIV*

This fruit of the spirit is a necessity because without love we wouldn't be here. *"We love because he first loved us." 1 John 4:19. NIV.*

How did he love us?

He loved us by giving up his one and only son. So that whoever believes in him would not be lost but have eternal life. God did not send his son into the world to judge the world guilty, but to **SAVE** the world through him. He who believes in God's son is not judged guilty. He who does not believe has already been judged guilty, because he has not believed in God's son. John 3:16-18 ERV.

How did he give up his son? Jesus (Son of God) died in our place to take away our sins. And Jesus is the way all people can have their sins taken away, too. 1 John 2:2 ERV.

According to the word of God in 1 Corinthians 13:4-7. ICB.

4 Love is patient and kind. Love is not jealous, it does not brag, and it is not proud. 5 Love is not rude, is not selfish, and does not become angry easily. Love does not remember wrongs done against it. 6 Love takes no pleasure in evil but rejoices over the truth. 7 Love patiently accepts all things. It always trusts, always hopes, and always continues strong.

Word of the lord

In your book tell them I AM the I AM for I know the plans I have for you. And they are GOOD. Your plans are bad they lead to destruction and hell on this earth. My plans lead to life and peace even in the midst of chaos. Trust me for I am trustworthy. Follow me for I will lead you along still waters. It is life in my word so that you may live. Stop trying to find me elsewhere. In my word you will find out everything you need to know. Don't try to exalt yourself up higher than your brothers and sisters by reading the lost books of the bible. Instead warn against them for they are not mines. My word is infallible and missing nothing. If you need more understanding, ask the Holy Spirit. Don't lean on research outside the word it is DANGEROUS. I beseech you to seek me for wisdom and guidance. I am here for you. I will teach you. Don't walk around confused because you are prideful. Because I am the bread of life. Ask and it will be given to you.

ShaRhonda D. Williams 38

Chapter 3

Joy

The Greek word for joy is Chairó- to be glad, to rejoice.

Biblical Definition of Joy

In the Bible, joy is more than just feeling happy; it's a deep, lasting sense of happiness that comes from our relationship with God. Here's what you need to know about biblical joy:

1. Joy in the Lord

   - Biblical joy comes from knowing and trusting God. It's not about our circumstances but about our connection with Him. Even when things aren't going well, joy can still be there because it's rooted in our relationship with God.

   Scripture: "The joy of the Lord is your strength" (Nehemiah 8:10).

2. Joy as a Fruit of the Spirit

- Joy is one of the fruits of the Spirit mentioned in Galatians. This means that true joy comes from following the Holy Spirit. It's not something we can create on our own; it grows in us when we follow God's lead.

Scripture: "The fruit of the Spirit is love, joy, peace..." (Galatians 5:22-23).

3. Joy in Tough Times

- The Bible says we can have joy even when we face difficulties. It's a sign of faith and hope, knowing that God is with us and working things out for our good. The bible promises us trials and tribulations but encourages us to let patience have it's perfect way because the testing of your faith produces endurance.

Scripture: "Consider it pure joy, my brothers and sisters, whenever you face trials of many kinds" (James 1:2-3).

4. Joy from Salvation

- Joy also comes from knowing that we are saved and have eternal life with God. It's about being thankful for the good news of salvation and the secure place we have in His kingdom.

Scripture: "Rejoice in the Lord always" (Philippians 4:4).

5. Joy as a Gift

- Joy is a special gift from God. It fills our hearts and minds with happiness that goes beyond what's happening around us.

Scripture: "You will fill me with joy in your presence" (Psalm 16:11).

In short, biblical joy is a deep, lasting happiness that comes from our relationship with God. It's not based on what's going on around us but on the peace and contentment we find in Him.

Picture this:

Every single day that you wake up on the foot of your bed is a gift awaiting you. How would that make you feel? What if other people didn't have that gift awaiting them at the foot of their bed? Would you only be concerned with having your gift? Did you know that the gift that you wake up to every single day is your life? Another chance to get right with God. One more chance to repent. Second chance to finish that book. Another chance to kiss your mom, kiss your kids, spouse, etc. Did you know that when you woke up this morning many people did not? So, they are the ones who did not receive that same gift? Instead of the gift of life they died and will be awaiting judgement day.

ShaRhonda D. Williams 41

Those reasons above are more than a reason to have joy. So just like the scripture says, today is the day that the Lord has made so rejoice in it and be glad! Psalm 118:24 NIV. Joy is a necessity because no matter what we endure in life we still have the precious gift of our life, and many don't. Be grateful.

Word of the Lord

For your book tell them this walk will not be easy and fiery thoughts will be thrown at you day and night. That's why I command you to be vigilant and to put on the full armor of God daily. Be ready for war because war is always happening. The adversary hates you and wants to destroy you. But stay in my will and he won't prevail. This is why you need my peace. The heat will turn up but you need to trust that's why it says peace that surpasses all understanding. That is the peace I leave with you beloved. You are my child in whom I love. I don't want you to fear but remember the scripture ye thou I walk through the valley of death I will fear no evil for thou art is with me. This entire world is evil. When you wake up and go to sleep your safety is in me. I will warn you, protect you, send my warrior angels out concerning you. Don't fret.

ShaRhonda D. Williams #3

Just like David fought Goliath will be you fighting the enemies of your soul. Every stronghold will come down, every false God will bow down. You are mines. AMEN.

Chapter 4

Peace

The Greek translation of peace is εἰρήνη 1.
State of national tranquility exemption from
rage and havoc of war. 2. Peace between
individuals, i.e., harmony. Concordance: one,
peace, quietness, rest.

Biblical Definition of Peace

In the Bible, peace is more than just the
absence of conflict or noise; it's a deep, inner
calm that comes from knowing and trusting
God. Here's what you need to know about
biblical peace:

1. Peace from God

   - Biblical peace comes from God and is
about having a calm heart and mind, no matter
what's going on around you. It's not something
we can make on our own; it's a gift from God.

Scripture: "The peace of God, which transcends all understanding, will guard your hearts and your minds in Christ Jesus" (Philippians 4:7).

2. Peace in Relationship with God

- True peace is found in a close relationship with God. When we trust Him and rely on His promises, we experience a peace that's deeper than just feeling good in the moment.

Scripture: "You will keep in perfect peace those whose minds are steadfast, because they trust in you" (Isaiah 26:3).

3. Peace in Difficult Times

- The Bible says that peace can still be present even when life is tough. It's about having a sense of calm and assurance that God is with us and working things out.

Scripture: "In this world you will have trouble. But take heart! I have overcome the world" (John 16:33).

4. Peace as a Fruit of the Spirit

- Peace is one of the fruits of the Spirit, meaning it's a quality that grows in us when we live according to the Holy Spirit. It's not something we can produce on our own but is a result of living closely with God.

Scripture: "The fruit of the Spirit is love, joy, peace..." (Galatians 5:22-23).

5. Peace through Forgiveness

- Peace also comes from forgiving others and letting go of bitterness. When we forgive, we free ourselves from anger and resentment, which brings inner peace.

Scripture: "Blessed are the peacemakers, for they will be called children of God" (Matthew 5:9).

In short, biblical peace is a deep, lasting calm that comes from knowing God and trusting in His plan. It's not just about avoiding problems but about having a steady, confident heart no matter what happens around us.

The best story of peace I could find in the scriptures was the story of Nabal and his wife Abigail, the peacemaker. Abigail is the best example of a wife who had her priorities in order, tenacity, and the influence to change the trajectory of her life. She could have used her influence to only save herself by running to hide because she was innocent. Instead, she courageously stood in the face of danger to save her family. This story in found in 1 Samuel 25 Nabal was a very rich man but he was evil in his doings. He had 3,000 sheep and 1,000 goats.

His wife was beautiful in appearance, wise, understanding, and humble. David sent young men up to Nabal in Carmel to speak in his name. They came kind and said peace be to you and your family. David's men told Nabal that they heard he was cutting the wool from his sheep. They mentioned that when his shepherds were with them at Carmel; they didn't harm them or steal anything from them. So, they asked Nabal to extend kindness to them. But Nabal responded and said, "Who is David?" Many have run away from their master's today! I have bread and water. And I have meat that I killed for my servants who cut the wool. But I won't give it to men I don't know. The men left and went to bring that message back to David. And David told them it's time for war then! Get your swords! We're taking it by force! David took 400 men and left 200 men behind with the supplies. Abigail caught wind of what was going on. Abigail was told that the men were good to Nabal's servants when they were in the field. Night and day, they protected them. They were like a wall around them. Trouble was coming for Nabal and his household because of how he disrespected David and his men. The servant said Nabal is an evil man, and no one can talk to him. Abigail rushed to gather 200 loaves of bread, 2 bags of wine, cakes, pressed figs. She put them on her animal and rode to meet David and the men. She had her servants go on, and she followed them. Abigail met David and his servant coming towards her home. Just before she came, David said this was a waste of time. I've been watching his home and none of his sheep were missing. He felt like he did right by Nabal, and they paid him back with wickedness.

21 David had just said, "It's been useless! I watched over Nabal's property in the desert. I made sure none of his sheep were missing. I did good to him, but he has paid me back with evil. 22 May God punish me terribly if I let just one of Nabal's family live until tomorrow." 23 When Abigail saw David, she quickly got off her donkey. She bowed facedown on the ground before David. 24 She lay at David's feet. She said, "My master, let the blame be on me! Please let me talk to you! Listen to what I say. 25 My master, don't pay attention to this worthless man Nabal. He is the same as his name. His name means 'fool,' and he is truly foolish. But I, your servant, didn't see the men you sent. 26 The Lord has kept you from killing and punishing people yourself. As surely as the Lord lives and

as surely as you live, may your enemies become like Nabal! [27] I have brought a gift to you. Please give it to the men who follow you. [28] Please forgive my wrong. The Lord will certainly let your family have many kings. He will do this because you fight his battles. As long as you live, people will find nothing bad in you. [29] A man might chase you to kill you. But the Lord your God will keep you alive. He will throw away your enemies' lives as he would throw a stone from a sling. [30] The Lord will keep all his promises about good things for you. He will make you leader over Israel. [31] Then you won't feel guilty. You won't have problems about killing innocent people and punishing them yourself. Please remember me when the Lord brings you success." 1 Samuel 25:22-35 ICB.

So, after that happened Abigail went home to her husband Nabal, who was drunk and happy. So, she didn't bother telling him she literally just begged to have his life spared. She waited until the morning to tell him. Then his heart failed him, and he died days later. When David got word that Nabal died, he rejoiced before the Lord. And he asked Abigail to be his wife. Abigail felt honored and accepted his proposal, becoming his 3rd wife at that time.

Abigail, much like Esther, she was willing to do whatever it took to save others, even if it was putting her own life in danger. If David said just a moment before she met him, that may the dealings of the Lord be with him if he let even just one member of Nabal's family live until the morning. And then she humbly fell to his feet being seconds away from being an innocent dead woman. Humility turns away wrath because David had murder on his mind because he felt disrespected, and he didn't care who lived at Nabal's house. But the gentleness, respect, honor, and bowing of Abigail spared Nabal's entire household. Because of his beautiful, wise, and understanding wife. Abigail was the epitome of a helpmate. Her husband was evil, but she was not, so she cleaned up what he messed up. Abigail was a peacemaker amid complete danger. All of those men with David with swords and she went before them by herself without her husband shows Proverbs 15:1 NIV true "A soft word turns away wrath, but a harsh word stirs up anger." Wise people learn from others; some learn only from their own experience; fools won't learn." NIV Nabal was the harsh word that stirred up wrath and almost got him killed. Abigail was the soft answer that turned away wrath and saved her foolish husband from death at the hands of David and his men.

Word Of The Lord

For your book tell them to seek me day and night. Tell them I am the bread of life. So, consume my word daily. Wake up and read the word of God. Do not stop renewing your mind with my word. It is vital. It is a fight for your life my anointed one. My word is a sword against the enemies camp. I will carry you. Don't fear. I am here and I will never leave nor forsake you. And don't forget to let go of whatever it is that is tormenting you. Forgive and let it go. Be free.

Chapter 5

Longsuffering / Patience

This fruit of the spirit has different names over the different translations. KJV and NKJV say long suffering. AMP, ERV, and ICB say patience.

The Greek word in which the New Testament was originally written in is makrothymia. Makrothymia is waiting for a sufficient time before expressing anger. This avoids the premature use of force (retribution) that rises out of improper anger. God showed Makrothymia (patience) in 2 Peter 3:15 NIV. "Bear in mind that our Lord's patience means salvation, just as our dear brother Paul also wrote with the wisdom that God gave him." It is a necessity because patience grows endurance and the ability to be content while waiting.

Biblical Definition of Long-Suffering/Patience

In the Bible, long-suffering (patience) is about being able to endure difficult situations and wait for things to improve without getting upset or giving up. Here's what you need to know:

1. Enduring Hardships

- Biblical patience means sticking with it during tough times. It's about not losing your cool or giving up when things are hard. It's a way of showing strong faith and trust in God even when things aren't going as planned.

Scripture: "Be patient, then, brothers and sisters, until the Lord's coming. See how the farmer waits for the land to yield its valuable crop, patiently waiting for the autumn and spring rains" (James 5:7).

2. Patient with Others

- Patience isn't just about enduring your own struggles; it's also about being patient with other people. It means dealing with others' faults or mistakes without getting frustrated or angry.

Scripture: "Be completely humble and gentle; be patient, bearing with one another in love" (Ephesians 4:2).

3. A Fruit of the Spirit
   - Patience is one of the fruits of the Spirit, which means it's something that grows in us when we're guided by the Holy Spirit. It's not something we can just force ourselves to have; it develops as we live closely with God.

Scripture: "The fruit of the Spirit is… patience" (Galatians 5:22-23).

4. Waiting on God's Timing
   - Biblical patience involves waiting on God's timing rather than trying to rush things. It's trusting that God knows what's best and will work things out in His perfect timing.

Scripture: "But if we hope for what we do not yet have, we wait for it patiently" (Romans 8:25).

5. Showing God's Character
   - Patience reflects God's own character. Just as God is patient with us, He wants us to show patience towards others, demonstrating His love and grace in our interactions.

Scripture: "The Lord is not slow in keeping his promise, as some understand slowness. Instead he is patient with you, not wanting anyone to perish, but everyone to come to repentance." (2 Peter 3:9).

In summary, biblical patience or long-suffering is about enduring difficult times, being patient with others, and waiting on God's timing. It's a quality that shows strong faith and trust in God, reflecting His own patience and love.

Picture this:

God is omnipresence. Keep that in mind. A mother had a son who was addicted to drugs. Before he got addicted to drugs, he bought them both a house next to each other. So, as he progresses in his addictions, she sees him. When he is hungry, she feeds him. When he needs clothing, she clothes him. When he needs to talk, she listens. But she also sees him talking to himself. She sees him starting fights and arguments. She even must referee between him and his brothers fighting. One day he breaks in her house and steals her jewelry and televisions. He breaks into another family member's house and steals from them. After that, he is arrested and sent to jail. She tries to be there for his children and their mothers while he's away. She sees how he's destroying his life. She feels angry, hopeless, and disappointed. Her wish is that when she dies, all her sons get along. That is a very simple wish. But how tormenting is it to watch your child that you birthed be strung out on drugs when he becomes a man?

Imagine how an omnipresent God feels. He sees all and he knows all. Yet he gave each of us freewill. So, just like parents say, their children are grown and can make their own choices. God allows us to make our own choices as well. And when we finally had enough of ruining our own life, we come with ashes, begging God to save us and help us. And he does!! That is long suffering. That is patience. God can snatch us up out of here at any moment. God can end it all. And of course, he wouldn't be wrong. Old school parents used to say if I brought you into this world, I could take you out. But God literally can take us out and he literally brought us in. Even the fact that God sent his son Jesus to die for our sins knowing that 2,000 years later, the same sinners he died for wouldn't choose him, believe in him, or love him back. They wouldn't appreciate the sacrifice God made so that they could live. That right there is true long-suffering/patience.

Chapter 6

Kindness

The greek word for kindness is *xrēstótēs* meaning goodness, excellence, uprightness. The word can be used for goodness, uprightness, kindness, gentleness. *Xrēstótēs* ("divine *kindness*") is the *Spirit-produced* goodness which meets the need and avoids human harshness (cruelty). "We have no term that quite carries this notion of *kind and good*."

Biblical Definition of Kindness

In the Bible, kindness is all about being genuinely good and caring towards others. It's not just about being polite or nice but showing real, heartfelt compassion and generosity. Here's what you need to know:

1. Being Good to Others
   - Biblical kindness means treating people with goodness and respect. It's about being thoughtful and considerate, looking out for others' needs, and acting with a generous spirit.

   Scripture: "Be kind and compassionate to one another, forgiving each other, just as in Christ God forgave you" (Ephesians 4:32).

2. Kindness in Actions
   - Kindness isn't just about saying kind words; it's also about doing kind things. It involves helping others, sharing with those in need, and being a source of support and comfort.

   Scripture: "Let us not become weary in doing good, for at the proper time we will reap a harvest if we do not give up" (Galatians 6:9).

3. A Fruit of the Spirit
   - Kindness is one of the fruits of the Spirit, which means it's a quality that grows in us when we live by the Holy Spirit. It's not just something we do on our own; it's a natural result of having the Spirit work in our lives.

Scripture: "The fruit of the Spirit is love, joy, peace, forbearance, kindness..." (Galatians 5:22-23).

4. Reflecting God's Love

- Biblical kindness reflects God's own love and character. Just as God shows kindness to us, He wants us to show that same kindness to others. It's a way of expressing His love through our actions.

Scripture: "But when the kindness and love of God our Savior appeared, he saved us... through the washing of rebirth and renewal by the Holy Spirit" (Titus 3:4-5).

5. Being Kind in Every Situation

- Kindness is not just for easy situations or people who are nice to us. It's about being kind to everyone, even when it's hard or when we're not treated well in return.

Scripture: "If your enemy is hungry, give him something to eat; if he is thirsty, give him something to drink" (Romans 12:20).

In summary, biblical kindness means genuinely caring for others, showing goodness through our actions, and reflecting God's love in how we treat people. It's a sign of living by the

Holy Spirit and being a true representative of God's character.

Picture this:

Have you ever driven down the service drive and seen a homeless person with a sign? What happens inside of you when you see that? Do you ignore them? Do you say hi? Do you look and see if you have anything for them? Or do you look to see if they're a fraud and have a nice car parked waiting for them after they're done begging? Kindness is even though you didn't plan to give or be bothered with someone in need you inconvenienced yourself to help. You ignore where you need to go, and go out of your way and buy them food and drinks and make the U-turn to take it back to them with a good attitude! You may not get a thank you or even a God bless you. But that is an act of kindness that may have inconvenienced you for all of 5 minutes. But who's to say that isn't the only meal they have today? And you were the one who blessed them with it! Even if they are a fraud in some way, would you be out there begging for anything from cars passing by? Do you think they are in a perfectly sound mind or perfect home situation? Regardless of your answer, bless them anyhow! Because honestly, it could always one day be you in need. This is merely a reasonable service. The bible tells us to help the poor. *"Blessed is he that considereth the poor: the Lord will deliver him in time of trouble." Psalm 41:1 KJV.*

Chapter 7

Goodness

The Greek word for goodness is agathosune, defined as doing good. The usage of the word is intrinsic goodness, especially as a personal quality, with stress on the kindly (rather than the righteous) side of goodness.

Biblical Definition of Goodness

In the Bible, goodness is about being morally upright and doing what's right. It's not just about being nice; it's about having a genuine, strong character that shows in your actions. Here's what you need to know:

1. Doing What's Right

   - Biblical goodness means making choices that align with God's standards and doing what's right, even when it's tough. It's about living with integrity and fairness in all you do.

Scripture: "Do not let any unwholesome talk come out of your mouths, but only what is helpful for building others up according to their needs." (Ephesians 4:29).

2. Being Upright and Honest

- Goodness involves being honest and upright in all your dealings. It's about being sincere and trustworthy, living a life that others can rely on.

Scripture: "The righteous lead blameless lives; blessed are their children after them." (Proverbs 20:7).

3. A Fruit of the Spirit

- Goodness is one of the fruits of the Spirit, which means it's a quality that grows in us when we live according to the Holy Spirit. It's not something we can just muster up on our own; it's a result of having the Spirit working in our lives.

Scripture: "The fruit of the Spirit is... goodness" (Galatians 5:22-23).

4. Reflecting God's Character

- Biblical goodness reflects the character of God. Just as God is good and does good things, He wants us to mirror that goodness in our own lives. It's about showing His love and righteousness through our actions.

Scripture: "The Lord is good to all; he has compassion on all he has made" (Psalm 145:9).

5. Acting with Generosity
   - Goodness also includes being generous and kind, looking for ways to help others and make their lives better. It's about going beyond just doing what's required and actively seeking to do good.

Scripture: "Brothers and sisters, never get tired of doing good." (2 Thessalonians 3:13). ERV

In summary, biblical goodness means living with integrity, honesty, and generosity. It's about making right choices, reflecting God's character, and letting the Holy Spirit work in your life to show goodness through your actions.

Story of Good Samaritan

Luke 10:29-37

A great story about goodness is the parable of the good Samaritan. A man was on his way from Jerusalem to Jericho, minding his own business. Then boom out of nowhere, he was ambushed, robbed and beaten within an inch of life. Just like today's culture, people saw him and walked right past him. Maybe they didn't want to be accused or simply didn't care. But then a Samaritan man saw him in such terrible shape and had instant compassion for him. He knew he had to help this man. So, he did what we would call today first aid by cleaning his wounds and bandaging him up. He put this man on his donkey and carried him to a hotel and paid for this man's stay. He paid for him to be taken care of, without desiring nothing in return just for the man to be well. He just knew this was right. He even said he would bring more money if needed. This is what Jesus meant by loving your neighbor as yourself. The good Samaritan saw the man lying in the road dying as his neighbor. Only love could make you show so much care and concern to a stranger. This is goodness and more is needed in this world.

ShaRhonda D. Williams 66

Chapter 8

Faithfulness

Biblical Definition of Faithfulness

In the Bible, faithfulness is about being loyal, reliable, and true to your commitments. It's not just about believing in God but also about sticking to your promises and being trustworthy in everything you do. Here's what you need to know:

1. Sticking to Your Commitments

   - Biblical faithfulness means being true to your word and keeping your promises, no matter what. It's about following through on your commitments and being dependable in all areas of life.

   Scripture: "Let love and faithfulness never leave you; bind them around your neck, write them on the tablet of your heart" (Proverbs 3:3).

2. Loyalty to God

- Faithfulness also means being loyal to God. It's about trusting Him, following His guidance, and staying committed to Him even when it's challenging.

Scripture: "If we are faithless, he remains faithful, for he cannot disown himself" (2 Timothy 2:13).

3. A Fruit of the Spirit

- Faithfulness is one of the fruits of the Spirit, which means it's a quality that grows in us when we live by the Holy Spirit. It's not something we can just force; it develops as we walk closely with God.

Scripture: "The fruit of the Spirit is... faithfulness" (Galatians 5:22-23).

4. Reflecting God's Reliability

- Biblical faithfulness mirrors God's own reliability. Just as God is always faithful and true to His promises, He wants us to reflect that same reliability and loyalty in our lives.

Scripture: "The Lord is trustworthy in all he promises and faithful in all he does." (Psalm 145:13).

5. Being Dependable in Relationships

- Faithfulness is important in our relationships with others. It means being someone others can count on, whether it's in friendships, family, or work. It's about showing integrity and trustworthiness in all your interactions.

Scripture: "A faithful person will be richly blessed, but one eager to get rich will not go unpunished." (Proverbs 28:20).

In summary, biblical faithfulness means being loyal and reliable in your commitments to God and others. It's about sticking to your promises, reflecting God's trustworthiness, and letting the Holy Spirit help you grow in faithfulness.

In relationships, we all want someone who is faithful to us. We want someone who chooses us. We want someone who is loyal to us even when nobody's looking and you're not around. The Greek word for faithfulness is pistis, which is to properly persuade, be persuaded, come to trust, faith.

Picture This:

You are married to a man who, when he's at work, he can't wait to get home to see you. You are married to a man who when he goes to lunch at work, he calls you just to hear your voice. You are married to a man who brings you flowers and chocolate when your period is making you feel gloomy. You are married to a man who says baby go lay down. I'll get the kids to bed and clean the kitchen. You are married to a man who even when people hate you, he loves you and defends you. You are married to a man who only has eyes for you. You are married to a man who wants to spend the rest of his life waking up to you. You are married to a man who sees you. You are married to a man who is committed to learning you. You are married to a man who hears you. You are married to a man who understands your unspoken words. You are married to a man who you can give a look to, and he knows you are uncomfortable, and he shuts it down. You are married to a man that women dream of being married to, but he doesn't look at them twice. You are married to a man who obeyed God and married you even though he didn't know you. This man is committed to you.

ShaRhonda D. Williams 70

Chapter 9

Gentleness

Gentleness is a necessity because it can help to restore someone who wanted to give up their will to live. Another word for gentleness is consideration, humility, meekness. In the Greek gentleness means cognate which expresses power with reserve and gentleness

"A gentle answer makes anger disappear, but a rough answer makes it grow." Proverbs 15: 1-2

Biblical Definition of Gentleness

In the Bible, gentleness is about being calm, kind, and considerate in how you interact with others. It's not about being weak but about having a gentle and respectful attitude that shows care and compassion. Here's what you need to know:

1. Being Kind and Respectful

- Biblical gentleness means treating others with kindness and respect. It's about speaking softly, being considerate of other people's feelings, and acting with care in all your interactions.

Scripture: "Let your gentleness be evident to all. The Lord is near." (Philippians 4:5).

2. A Fruit of the Spirit

- Gentleness is one of the fruits of the Spirit, which means it's a quality that grows in us when we live by the Holy Spirit. It's not something we can just force; it develops as we walk closely with God.

Scripture: "The fruit of the Spirit is... gentleness" (Galatians 5:22-23).

3. Handling Others with Care

- Gentleness involves handling others with care and avoiding harshness. It means responding with patience and understanding, even when someone is difficult or when you're dealing with a challenging situation.

Scripture: "A gentle answer turns away wrath, but a harsh word stirs up anger" (Proverbs 15:1).

4. Reflecting Christ's Character

- Biblical gentleness reflects the character of Jesus. He was gentle and humble, even when facing tough situations. He wants us to show that same gentleness in our own lives.

Scripture: "Take my yoke upon you and learn from me, for I am gentle and humble in heart, and you will find rest for your souls" (Matthew 11:29).

5. Being Gentle in Correction

- Gentleness also means being careful and loving when you correct or guide others. It's about offering advice or correction in a way that's helpful and caring, rather than harsh or judgmental.

Scripture: "Brothers and sisters, if someone is caught in a sin, you who live by the Spirit should restore that person gently"(Galatians 6:1).

In summary, biblical gentleness is about being kind, respectful, and caring in how you treat others. It's a sign of living by the Holy Spirit and reflecting Jesus' character in your interactions.

Picture this:

What if your sister randomly said she understands why people commit suicide? She says, Life is so hard, and they just couldn't handle it anymore. They weren't good enough and never will be. You tell your sister to stop it. That's stupid talk. People who commit suicide are selfish and stupid because everyone else will suffer who they left.

You are trying to reason with her about how she's wrong in her thinking. You sincerely want your sister to understand that the way she's thinking is wrong. That she's making excuses for them that would never heal their mother's broken heart when she must bury that child she birthed. But she starts to yell and talk to you aggressively. She says, you don't understand sister, it's how they really feel. You just have an easy, perfect life! Everyone does not. Then you talk to her aggressively and the conversation just turns heated, and it loses control. You yell at your sister, what are you talking about? Are you insane? We had the same life! We have the same biological parents who loved and raised us! Are you drunk? You know what sister I'm done with this conversation. Then you storm off and leave. An hour later, you get a hysterical call that your sister was found hanging from her bedroom ceiling fan dead. That someone she was talking to you about who she understood why they wanted to commit suicide, was her. She left a note behind saying that she was sorry she had to go because she got an abortion a week before and could not deal with the guilt anymore. Gentleness is needed.

Chapter 10

Self Control

Self-control is life control because it will save your life. Anger, pride, greed, and control can lead to murder.

The perfect story of losing self-control was the story about Mitchelle Blair. A true story about a woman from Detroit, Michigan, who believed her daughter and son were molesting/raping her youngest son. So, she snapped and ultimately killed the two older children. She said I told my kids I was raped and that's the worst thing you can do to a person. She tortured them, and hid their bodies in a deep freezer in her living room for 3 years. They were only found because she was evicted, and they found the decayed bodies during the eviction. She claims she felt justified because she avenged her son. Now she serves life in prison with no possibility of parole without any of her 4 children. Lack of self-control destroyed her and her children's life forever.

Self-control will keep you out of sin. Because if you don't control yourself, you will give in to the lust of the flesh whenever the opportunity presents itself. Lack of self-control is of the devil. It is unhinged, self-seeking, unsafe, unfruitful, dangerous, detrimental, prideful. It stems from Jezebel. She is unhinged. She goes on a rampage and destroys everything in her path. Self-control is the ability to control oneself. It doesn't matter if you are angry, scared, sad, happy, depressed, confused, lost. You will always have to deal with the consequences of losing control of yourself. Just like you would if you lost control of your car and hit people. Your reactions show yourself control or lack thereof. Our words and hands can harm someone just like that out of control car. That's why the bible commands us in James 1:19 to be slow to speak, slow to anger, instead be quick to listen. And to not have feet that are quick to run to evil. Proverbs 6:18 Self-control will help you walk in the other fruits of the spirit, which are love, joy, peace, patience, faithfulness, goodness, kindness, and gentleness. If we obey the scriptures, we will learn to guard our hearts for the issues of life flow out of them. That will help us know to guard our ears what we allow into our temples through listening. We need to start with controlling our tongues, so we don't curse and bless out the same mouth. Then control our eyes because if you lust after someone in your heart, you already committed adultery.

Biblical Definition of Self-Control

In the Bible, self-control is all about managing your impulses and desires, making sure they don't control you. It means having the discipline to choose what's right and avoid giving in to unhealthy or harmful behaviors.

Here's what you need to know:

1. Managing Your Impulses
   - Biblical self-control means being able to control your urges and impulses. It's about making thoughtful decisions instead of acting on the spur of the moment. It's a key part of living a disciplined and godly life.

Scripture: "Like a city whose walls are broken through is a person who lacks self-control" (Proverbs 25:28).

2. A Fruit of the Spirit

- Self-control is one of the fruits of the Spirit. This means it's something that grows in us when we live by the Holy Spirit. It's not just something we can develop on our own; it's a result of the Spirit working in our lives.

Scripture: "The fruit of the Spirit is... self-control" (Galatians 5:22-23).

3. Disciplining Yourself

- Self-control involves disciplining yourself to avoid things that could lead you astray or harm you. It's about having the strength to say no to things that aren't good for you and making choices that align with God's will.

Scripture: "Everyone who competes in the games goes into strict training. They do it to get a crown that will not last; but we do it to get a crown that will last forever" (1 Corinthians 9:25).

4. Reflecting God's Strength
- Biblical self-control reflects God's strength and power in your life. Just as God has the power to help us overcome challenges, He wants us to show that same strength in controlling our own desires and actions.
Scripture: "For God gave us a spirit not of fear but of power and love and self-control" (2 Timothy 1:7).

5. Keeping Your Focus
- Self-control helps keep your focus on what's important. It means staying committed to your goals and values, rather than getting sidetracked by distractions or temptations.
Scripture: "Do you not know that in a race all the runners run, but only one gets the prize? Run in such a way as to get the prize" (1 Corinthians 9:24).

In summary, biblical self-control is about managing your impulses and making disciplined choices. It's a fruit of the Spirit that helps you live a focused and godly life, reflecting God's strength and maintaining control over your actions and desires.

Word of The
Lord

God said for your book tell the people don't get weary in well doing, for the scriptures say you will reap a harvest if you don't give up. I am the prince of peace. I will give you peace if you seek me and ask me. Don't you know my word says I would not withhold a good thing from you? That includes you. Don't get led astray by all the new practices. Stay the course and be obedient to my voice and read my word for understanding. If you have a bad feeling about someone, it is an unction from the holy spirit to warn you of danger. So be cautious, vigilant, and prayerful. Don't trust every person who calls themselves my sheep. My sheep heed my voice. So, if you want to be mines you have to give up your life, selfish ambitious, take up your cross and follow Christ.

ShaRhonda D. Williams 81

To the divorcees, you are not casted out. You are not the black sheep of the family. Your sin is just as ugly as another's. As long as you repented, you are forgiven. But don't encourage others to divorce. Encourage them to work their marriage out, pray for them, fast for them, cry out to God for them. You know the heartbreak you experienced. Don't push that on another. Instead, give them hope that they can make it and win their spouse over. Just like if a murderer got off on a murder, he was guilty. Should we encourage others to murder because they will get away with it too? Heavens no. So, you think the same of your sin that you were forgiven for.

Chapter 11

Fruits Of The Flesh

The fruit of the flesh is sin, and it is our default setting. We were born into sin because of what happened between Adam and Eve in the garden. However, when we are born again believers, we need to let the fruits of the flesh die every day. *"For though we walk in the flesh, we do not war according to the flesh. For the weapons of our warfare are not carnal but mighty in God for pulling down strongholds, casting down arguments and every high thing that exalts itself against the knowledge of God, bringing every thought into captivity to the obedience of Christ, and being ready to punish* all disobedience when your obedience is fulfilled." 2 Corinthians 10 NKJV.

How do we not walk in the fruit of the flesh but in the fruit of the spirit instead?

First, we need to know what the fruit of the flesh is. In chapters 2-10, we discussed the fruits of the spirit and their necessity, which for contrast's sake; are love, joy, peace, patience, goodness, gentleness, faithfulness, kindness, self-control.

The fruits of the flesh are simple committing sexual sins, being morally bad, doing all kind of shameful things, worshipping false god's, witchcraft, hatred, being a trouble starter, jealousy, causing division amongst people, enviousness (resentful and painful awareness of another's advantages), being drunk, having wild parties. These fruits of the flesh are found in Galatians 5:19-21. The scriptures say those who participate in these things will not inherit the kingdom of God. Inherit means to receive something that you did nothing to receive because you are an heir. An heir is usually a spouse or child of. In this case, we would be considered children of God. He has this kingdom with everything you ever needed and ever wanted, that he wants to freely give to you.

Biblical Definition of Fruits of the Flesh

In the Bible, the "fruits of the flesh" are behaviors and attitudes that come from our sinful nature. These are things we do when we're not living by the Spirit but are letting our own desires and impulses take over. Here's what you need to know:

1. Self-Centered Actions
   - The fruits of the flesh are all about actions and attitudes that focus on ourselves and what we want, rather than what God wants. They come from a place of selfishness and often lead to hurt and conflict.
   Scripture: "The acts of the flesh are obvious: sexual immorality, impurity and debauchery" (Galatians 5:19).

2. Behaviors That Hurt Others
   - These fruits often include things that harm our relationships with others. Things like anger, jealousy, and strife are examples of how

the flesh can lead us to act in ways that damage our connections with people.

Scripture: "Hatred, discord, jealousy, fits of rage, selfish ambition, dissensions, factions" (Galatians 5:20).

3. Lack of Self-Control

- One of the marks of the fruits of the flesh is a lack of self-control. When we're driven by the flesh, we often struggle to manage our impulses and desires, leading to behaviors that are not aligned with God's ways.

Scripture: "Drunkenness, orgies, and the like" (Galatians 5:21).

4. Opposite of the Fruits of the Spirit

- The fruits of the flesh are the opposite of the fruits of the Spirit. Where the fruits of the Spirit are about love, joy, and peace, the fruits of the flesh are about things that cause division and conflict.

Scripture: "But the fruit of the Spirit is love, joy, peace, forbearance, kindness, goodness, faithfulness, gentleness and self-control" (Galatians 5:22-23).

5. Living by the Flesh

- Living according to the flesh means letting these negative behaviors and attitudes guide you. It's a sign that you're not fully living in the freedom and guidance that comes from the Holy Spirit.

Scripture: "Those who belong to Christ Jesus have crucified the flesh with its passions and desires" (Galatians 5:24).

In summary, the fruits of the flesh are behaviors and attitudes that come from our sinful nature. They are self-centered and harmful to our relationships with others, and they stand in contrast to the positive qualities that come from living by the Holy Spirit.

Chapter 12

Sexual

Immorality

God created sex for a purpose. It was to be used between husband and wife to produce life. They produce life by conceiving and the wife bears a child that turns into an adult like you reading this book. The purpose of sex was never merely only for our pleasure, pain, abuse, control, manipulation, and financial gain. It was originally designed for us to indulge in between one man and one woman who are married under a covenant with God to be fruitful and multiply on the earth. Sex has been perverted and used in despicable ways that God hates, and in other ways God calls an abomination, which means disgraceful and evil. If you find yourself in any of these sins, no matter how much shame, anger, and confusion wants to come upon, you simply repent. Repent means to change your mind and turn away the sin. Repentance comes from renewing your mind with the word of God. We don't know what we don't know until we find out. So, no need to walk in shame, anger, or confusion any longer. Repentance is for the believer. It is not over for you if you committed these sins. The choice lies in your hands, do you want to give these up to obey Christ? You're not condemned to hell with no way out if you make a choice before you die or even if you made a mistake since you first got saved. Repentance is a choice to change your mind and desert those sins you used to love to obey God. Repentance needs to be a daily discipline. The more you learn in the word of God, the more you should be repenting. In the last chapter will be a breakdown with steps on how to be free.

What is considered sexual immorality?

Biblical Definition of Sexual Immorality

In the Bible, sexual immorality covers a range of behaviors that go against God's design for sexuality. It's about any sexual activity that is outside the boundaries set by God. Here's what you need to know:

1. Going Against God's Design
    - Sexual immorality means engaging in sexual behaviors that don't match up with what God says is right. It's about any kind of sexual activity that's outside the marriage relationship between a man and a woman.
        Scripture: "Run from sexual immorality. All other sins a person commits are outside the body, but whoever sins sexually, sins against their own body" (1 Corinthians 6:18).

2. Includes Various Behaviors
    - This term includes a variety of behaviors such as adultery (cheating on your spouse), fornication (sex outside of marriage), and other sexual practices that go against God's guidelines.

Scripture: "You shall not commit adultery" (Exodus 20:14).

3. Not Just Physical Actions
- Sexual immorality isn't just about physical actions; it also includes wrong thoughts and attitudes toward sex. It's about keeping your heart and mind in line with God's standards.

Scripture: "But I tell you that anyone who looks at a woman lustfully has already committed adultery with her in his heart" (Matthew 5:28).

4. Impact on Relationships
- Engaging in sexual immorality can hurt relationships and cause personal and emotional harm. It's a sign of not following God's plan for healthy and loving relationships.

Scripture: "Marriage should be honored by all, and the marriage bed kept pure, for God will judge the adulterer and all the sexually immoral" (Hebrews 13:4).

5. Living a Pure Life
- The Bible calls us to live a pure and holy life, which includes avoiding sexual immorality.

It's about aligning your actions and thoughts with God's design for sexuality.

Scripture: "It is God's will that you should be sanctified: that you should avoid sexual immorality" (1 Thessalonians 4:3).

In summary, biblical sexual immorality refers to any sexual activity that goes against God's design and guidelines. It includes physical actions and wrong attitudes, and it impacts relationships and personal well-being. The Bible encourages us to live a pure and holy life, staying true to God's standards for sexuality.

We will break it completely down in several categories.

We are not under the Old Testament law since Jesus came and died for our sins making a new covenant. However, he still gave guidelines on how we're supposed to live as Christians in the New Testament. The fruits of the flesh are in Galatians, which are the New Testament, and the Old Testament explains what they are. The New Testament was written in Greek so you can look up words. Old Testament was written in Hebrew. If you don't accept Jesus as your Lord and savior, repent for your sins, then you are not covered under the blood of Jesus. In that case, you are under the law and judgment is upon you. The bible says in the New Testament to keep the commandments.

LUST is impure thoughts, desires, motives feelings, uncontrollable urges, and dreams of sex. If you undress people with your eyes and daydream about having sex with them. You find yourself staring lustfully at their body parts. The bible says if you look upon a woman lustfully, you have already committed adultery in your heart.

In the Bible, lust refers to strong, wrongful desires, especially when it comes to sexual attraction. It's not just about feeling attracted to someone; it's about having intense and uncontrolled cravings that lead you away from what God wants. Here's what you need to know:

1. **Intense Desires**

- Lust is about having powerful, often unhealthy desires. It's not just a fleeting attraction but a deep and intense craving that goes beyond normal feelings.

2. **Scripture**: *"But I tell you that anyone who looks at a woman lustfully has already committed adultery with her in his heart"* (Matthew 5:28).

3. **Beyond Physical Attraction**

- While it includes physical attraction, lust goes further into obsession and impurity. It's about focusing on someone in a way that is not pure or respectful.

4. **Scripture**: *"Do not lust in your heart after her beauty or let her captivate you with her eyes"* (Proverbs 6:25).

5. **Leading to Sin**

- Lust can lead to sinful actions and behaviors. It's a powerful force that can drive you to make choices that are against God's commands and damage relationships.

6. **Scripture**: *"Each person is tempted when they are dragged away by their own evil desire and enticed"* (James 1:14).

7. **Controlling Your Thoughts**

- The Bible teaches that lust is also about what's going on in your mind and heart. It's important to manage your thoughts and desires to stay aligned with God's standards.

8. **Scripture**: *"For from within, out of the heart, come evil thoughts, sexual*

immorality, theft, murder, adultery" (Mark 7:21).

9. **Seeking Purity**

● To overcome lust, the Bible encourages us to seek purity and focus on what is good and honorable. It's about aligning your desires with God's will and living a life of integrity.

10. **Scripture**: *"Flee from sexual immorality. All other sins a person commits are outside the body, but whoever sins sexually, sins against their own body"* (1 Corinthians 6:18).

In summary, biblical lust refers to intense and wrongful desires, especially of a sexual nature. It goes beyond mere attraction and can lead to sinful actions. The Bible calls us to manage our thoughts and desires, seeking purity and aligning our actions with God's will.

Perversion is **ekstrephó: to turn inside out, fig. to pervert. A change for the worse, To pervert, corrupt.** Perversion is an unnatural desire for unnatural things and improper use of something. Perversion is uncontrollable lust. Such things are *addiction to pornography*. Using sex toys and objects to pleasure yourself or others.

God calls incest, abortion (sacrificing children to Molech), bestiality, and homosexuality an abomination meaning it is disgraceful. Refer to Leviticus 18 and Leviticus 20. *Homosexuality* which is men having sex with men. Women having sex with women. Be reminded that you can repent (make a choice to walk away from it) and renounce homosexuality. It is a spirit that wants to ruin your life, confuse you, and make you prideful. However, if you decide to turn away from it and renounce it and go through deliverance. All of what you did can be forgiven because that is why Christ died for our sins. You can be made right with Christ.

In the Bible, perversion refers to twisting or corrupting what is right and pure, especially in relation to moral and sexual behavior. It's about distorting God's original design and engaging in behaviors that go against His standards. Here's what you need to know:

11. Distortion of What is Good

- Perversion means taking something that was originally good and twisting it into something harmful or sinful. It's about corrupting God's intentions for how we should live and act.

12.   **Scripture**: *"They have become corrupt; their deeds are vile; there is no one who does good"* (Psalm 14:1).

13.   **Unnatural Behaviors**

• In terms of sexual behavior, perversion often refers to practices that are considered unnatural or outside of God's design for sexuality. It's about engaging in sexual activities that are not aligned with biblical teachings.

14.   **Scripture**: *"Do not have sexual relations with a man as one does with a woman; that is detestable"* (Leviticus 18:22).

15.   **Moral Corruption**

• Perversion also includes a general moral corruption, where actions and attitudes are not just wrong but are a complete departure from what is right and true according to God's Word.

16.   **Scripture**: *"They have become corrupt and done abominable deeds; there is none who does good"* (Psalm 53:3).

17.   **Impact on Relationships and Society**

- Engaging in perverted behaviors can damage relationships and have a negative impact on society. It disrupts God's order and can lead to greater harm and confusion.

18.　　**Scripture**: *"Woe to those who call evil good and good evil, who put darkness for light and light for darkness, who put bitter for sweet and sweet for bitter"* (Isaiah 5:20).

19.　　**Call to Purity**

- The Bible calls us to reject perversion and seek purity. It's about aligning our lives with God's standards and living in a way that honors Him and reflects His goodness.

20.　　**Scripture**: *"But among you there must not be even a hint of sexual immorality, or of any kind of impurity"* (Ephesians 5:3).

In summary, biblical perversion is about twisting what is good and pure into something corrupt and sinful. It involves engaging in behaviors that are contrary to God's design and leads to moral and societal harm. The Bible calls us to reject perversion and strive for purity in all areas of our lives.

Cross dressing men dressing like women and women dressing like men. Being *effeminate* which is when a male is having some characteristic of a woman, as delicacy, luxuriousness, etc.; soft or delicate to an unmanly degree; womanish; weak. The bible says that they will not inherit the kingdom of God.

In the Bible, cross-dressing refers to wearing clothing that is typically associated with the opposite gender. It's mentioned in the context of following God's design for gender roles and avoiding practices that could be seen as confusing or contrary to His intentions. Here's what you need to know:

21. **Wearing Clothes of the Opposite Gender**

- Cross-dressing means wearing clothes that are generally considered appropriate for the opposite sex. In biblical terms, this practice is addressed as something that goes against the traditional roles and distinctions God has set.

22. **Scripture**: *"A woman must not wear men's clothing, nor a man wear women's clothing, for the Lord*

your God detests anyone who does this"
(Deuteronomy 22:5).

23.   **Respecting   Gender
Distinctions**

- The Bible highlights the importance of maintaining clear distinctions between male and female roles and appearances. This is seen as part of respecting and upholding God's design for gender.

24.   **Scripture**:   *"So   God
created mankind in his own image, in
the image of God he created them; male
and female he created them"* (Genesis
1:27).

25.   **Cultural and Religious
Context**

- In biblical times, cross-dressing was associated with cultural practices that were often tied to idolatry or religious rituals that were not in line with God's commands. The Bible warns against adopting such practices.

26.   **Scripture**: *"When you
enter the land the Lord your God is
giving you, do not learn to imitate the*

detestable ways of the nations there"
(Deuteronomy 18:9).

27.   **Understanding   the
Principle**

• The   principle   behind   the
prohibition is about maintaining clarity
in gender roles and avoiding confusion or
practices that might lead away from
God's design. It's about aligning with
God's order and purpose.

28.   **Scripture**: *"The Lord is
not a God of disorder but of peace"* (1
Corinthians 14:33).

29.   **Seeking   God's
Guidance**

• If you have questions or struggles
regarding gender and dress, the Bible
encourages seeking God's guidance and
understanding His design. It's about
living in a way that honors Him and
aligns with His teachings.

30.   **Scripture**: *"If any of you
lacks wisdom, you should ask God, who
gives generously to all without finding
fault, and it will be given to you"* (James
1:5).

In summary, biblical cross-dressing refers to wearing clothing associated with the opposite gender and is seen as contrary to God's design for clear gender distinctions. The Bible encourages maintaining these distinctions and seeking to align with God's order and purpose.

Pedophilia, which is any rape, molestation, attraction to a child. Because a child is not of age to ever consent rather you are the opposite gender or the same gender. Pedophilia is a very evil and despicable thing done unto innocent children used to damage them and steal their identity before they ever had a chance to choose for themselves.

In the Bible, pedophilia involves inappropriate sexual behavior or attraction toward children. This is clearly against God's standards and teachings. Here's what you need to know:

31.   Inappropriate Behavior Towards Children

- Pedophilia refers to sexual attraction or behavior directed at children, which is completely wrong according to biblical standards and moral standards. The Bible is clear that such actions are sinful and harmful.

32.   **Scripture**: *"But if anyone causes one of these little ones—those who believe in me—to stumble, it would be better for them to have a large millstone hung around their neck and to be drowned in the depths of the sea"* (Matthew 18:6).

33.   **Protecting   the Vulnerable**

- The Bible emphasizes protecting and caring for children. It is a serious offense to exploit or harm them in any way. Children are seen as precious and are to be treated with love and respect.

34.   **Scripture**: *"Children are a heritage from the Lord, offspring a reward from him"* (Psalm 127:3).

35.   **Moral   and   Ethical Standards**

- Engaging in or condoning pedophilia goes against the moral and ethical standards set by God. It is a severe violation of God's commands and is considered deeply sinful.

36.   **Scripture**: *"Woe to the world because of the things that cause people to stumble! Such things must*

come, but woe to the person who causes
them" (Matthew 18:7).

37.   **God's Justice**

• The Bible speaks of God's justice
and His judgment on those who commit
such grievous sins. Pedophilia is viewed
as an act of severe injustice and is
condemned in the Bible.

38.   **Scripture**: *"The Lord is a
refuge for the oppressed, a stronghold in
times of trouble"* (Psalm 9:9).

39.   **Call to Righteousness**

• The Bible calls us to live
righteously and uphold God's standards.
This includes rejecting any form of sexual
immorality and protecting those who are
vulnerable, especially children.

40.   **Scripture**: *"Finally, be
strong in the Lord and in his mighty
power"* (Ephesians 6:10).

In summary, biblical pedophilia refers to
any sexual attraction or behavior towards
children, which is considered sinful and
unacceptable according to God's standards. The
Bible emphasizes protecting and respecting
children and upholding moral and ethical
behavior.

Bestiality is any oral sex given or received by an animal. Animals should not be licking your genitals or anus. Any penetration or trying to penetrate an animal this is too unnatural. Animals are not made for your pleasure and to be a sex slave unto a human. This is an example of uncleanness is a person having sex with any kind of animal.

In the Bible, bestiality refers to sexual activity between humans and animals. This practice is clearly forbidden and is considered a serious sin. Here's what you need to know:

41.   **Sexual Activity with Animals**

- Bestiality means engaging in sexual acts with animals, which is explicitly prohibited in the Bible. It's seen as a gross violation of God's design for human sexuality.

42.   **Scripture**: *"Do not have sexual relations with an animal and defile yourself with it. A woman must not present herself to an animal to have sexual relations with it; that is a perversion"* (Leviticus 18:23).

43.   **Against God's Design**

- The Bible teaches that sexual activity is meant to be within the bounds of marriage between a man and a woman. Bestiality goes against this design and is seen as corrupt and unnatural.

44.　**Scripture**:　*"Marriage should be honored by all, and the marriage bed kept pure, for God will judge the adulterer and all the sexually immoral"* (Hebrews 13:4).

45.　**Moral and Ethical Standards**

- Engaging in bestiality is not only against God's laws but also against basic moral and ethical standards. It is seen as a form of sexual immorality that defies the created order.

46.　**Scripture**: *"You shall not lie with a male as with a woman. It is an abomination"* (Leviticus 18:22).

47.　**Sin and Purity**

- The Bible emphasizes living a pure and holy life. Bestiality is considered a serious sin that defiles and corrupts. It is strongly condemned as part of living in righteousness.

48. **Scripture**: *"Flee from sexual immorality. All other sins a person commits are outside the body, but whoever sins sexually, sins against their own body"* (1 Corinthians 6:18).

49. **Call to Righteousness**

• The Bible calls us to uphold God's standards for sexuality and reject any form of immorality, including bestiality. It's about living in a way that honors God's design and commands.

50. **Scripture**: *"Finally, be strong in the Lord and in his mighty power"* (Ephesians 6:10).

In summary, biblical bestiality refers to any sexual activity between humans and animals, which is strictly forbidden in the Bible. It's seen as a serious sin against God's design for sexuality and is condemned as part of living a pure and righteous life.

Fornication is two non-married people having sex with each other. The bible says that if you can't control yourself, then you ought to marry. Let each man have his own wife and each woman have her own husband.

Under the umbrella of fornication may lead to a surprise pregnancy or unplanned pregnancy. If you find yourself contemplating on if you should abort your baby or not. Hear this, a surprise to you isn't a surprise to God. What may have been meant for bad can be used for your good. You don't have to hide your sin from people because God already knows. God died so you could repent for your sins. Will you still have to deal with a consequence? Yes. But it doesn't have to be as severe as what we truly deserve for sinning. You don't have to hide from your responsibility from the child God placed in your womb. Even if it is hard you can do it. May you make better decisions because of it. You don't have to abort your baby because you can't afford it, or you don't want the baby, or the other parent doesn't want it. If you are a believer especially remember that even in your irresponsible choice God still loves you and he loves that innocent baby as well. God can help you take care of your baby if you pray and ask him too. Just know that you are not alone. Many of your brothers and sisters made the same irresponsible decisions and they are dealing with those consequences. Some made the decision to abort their child that they will never be able to change. Some regret it and are tortured at night. Some don't and believe it was the best decision that they made at the moment. But I challenge you to care about what God feels about the decisions that you make and to consult him about all things. He cares for you.

In the Bible, fornication refers to sexual activity between people who are not married to each other. It's considered sinful because it goes against God's design for sex and relationships. Here's what you need to know:

1. Sex Outside of Marriage

- Fornication is any kind of sexual activity between individuals who are not married. The Bible teaches that sex is meant to be enjoyed within the commitment of marriage between a man and a woman.

Scripture: "Flee from sexual immorality. All other sins a person commits are outside the body, but whoever sins sexually, sins against their own body." (1 Corinthians 6:18).

2. Against God's Design

- The Bible sets clear boundaries for sexual activity, placing it within the context of marriage. Fornication falls outside of these boundaries and is seen as a violation of God's plan for human relationships.

Scripture: "Marriage should be honored by all, and the marriage bed kept pure, for God will judge the adulterer and all the sexually immoral" (Hebrews 13:4).

3. Moral and Spiritual Implications

- Fornication is not just a physical act; it has moral and spiritual consequences. It's considered a form of sexual immorality that affects your relationship with God and can lead to spiritual harm.

Scripture: "You know that the wicked will not inherit the kingdom of God. Do not be deceived: Neither the sexually immoral nor idolaters nor adulterers nor men who have sex with men" (1 Corinthians 6:9).

4. Call to Purity

- The Bible calls us to live in purity and avoid sexual immorality. This includes abstaining from fornication and aligning our sexual behavior with God's standards.

Scripture: "It is God's will that you should be sanctified: that you should avoid sexual immorality." (1 Thessalonians 4:3).

5. Living According to God's Commands

- Following God's commands means respecting His design for sexuality and relationships. Fornication is seen as a departure from this design and is something to be avoided.

Scripture: "Finally, be strong in the Lord and in his mighty power" (Ephesians 6:10).

In summary, biblical fornication refers to any sexual activity outside of marriage, which is considered sinful according to God's design. The Bible encourages us to avoid fornication and live in purity, aligning our actions with God's standards for relationships and sexuality.

Adultery *i*s having sex with a married woman/man. Or having sex with someone other than your spouse. This is out of order. You are married if you're separated. You are married if you just moved out of your spouse's house. You are married if your spouse abandoned you. The person you are legally married to is who you are legally permitted to have sex with to still be in right standing with God. This sin people were stoned for in the Old Testament. Consider today's society, many spouses are killing their spouses for cheating because this ought not be. Adultery is heart breaking and tears apart a family. It destroys a family that may have produced children. But remember, you can repent, meaning to change your mind.

In the Bible, adultery is when someone who is married has a sexual relationship with someone who is not their spouse. It's seen as a serious sin because it breaks the trust and commitment of marriage. Here's what you need to know:

1. Cheating on Your Spouse

- Adultery means being unfaithful to your spouse by having a sexual relationship with someone else. The Bible is clear that this breaks the marriage covenant and is a serious wrongdoing.

Scripture: "You shall not commit adultery" (Exodus 20:14).

2. Breaking the Marriage Covenant

- Marriage is meant to be a committed and exclusive relationship between a husband and wife. Adultery violates this commitment and goes against the promises made in marriage.

Scripture: "What God has joined together, let no one separate." (Mark 10:9).

3. Impact on Relationships

- Adultery harms not only the marriage relationship but also affects families and communities. It creates trust issues and emotional pain, and goes against the principles of faithfulness and integrity.

Scripture: "The man who commits adultery is an utter fool, for he destroys himself." (Proverbs 6:32).

4. Moral and Spiritual Consequences

- The Bible teaches that adultery has moral and spiritual consequences. It's seen as a form of sexual immorality that impacts your relationship with God and can lead to spiritual harm.

Scripture: "Marriage should be honored by all, and the marriage bed kept pure, for God will judge the adulterer and all the sexually immoral." (Hebrews 13:4).

5. Call to Faithfulness

- The Bible calls us to be faithful in our marriages and to uphold the sanctity of the marital relationship. Avoiding adultery means honoring your spouse and living according to God's design for marriage.

Scripture: "Let marriage be held in honor among all, and let the marriage bed be undefiled." (Hebrews 13:4).

In summary, biblical adultery refers to a married person having sexual relations with someone other than their spouse. It is a serious sin that breaks the trust and commitment of marriage, with significant moral and spiritual consequences. The Bible encourages faithfulness and upholding the sanctity of marriage.

Lewdness is indecency or obscenity, vulgar sexual character or behavior. So, things like prostituting yourself on the street corners, creating sex videos, and stripping in clubs. We know it's illegal to walk around naked in broad daylight. It is called indecent exposure. You can be ticketed and made to spend 180 days in jail. Likewise, with selling your body on the street corner. If caught, you can be ticketed and jailed.

In the Bible, lewdness refers to behavior that is openly sexual, crude, or morally corrupt. It's about acting in a way that is shameless and goes against God's standards for purity and decency. Here's what you need to know:

1. Shameless Behavior
- Lewdness means behaving in a way that is openly sexual or indecent. It's about acting without regard for modesty or respect, and it often involves crude or inappropriate actions.
Scripture: "The acts of the flesh are obvious: sexual immorality, impurity and debauchery"(Galatians 5:19).

2. Corruption and Immorality
- Lewdness involves moral corruption and a lack of self-control. It's seen as part of a

broader pattern of sexual immorality and impure behavior that goes against God's design for how we should live.

Scripture: "So I tell you that you must no longer live as the Gentiles do, in the futility of their thinking"* (Ephesians 4:17).

3. Impact on Others
- Engaging in lewdness can negatively impact others by promoting inappropriate behavior and attitudes. It can lead to further immorality and damage relationships by fostering a culture of disrespect and impurity.

Scripture: "Do not let any unwholesome talk come out of your mouths, but only what is helpful for building others up according to their needs" (Ephesians 4:29)

4. Call to Purity
- The Bible calls us to avoid lewdness and instead pursue purity and holiness. It's about living in a way that reflects God's standards and honoring Him with our actions and thoughts.

Scripture: "Finally, brothers and sisters, whatever is true, whatever is noble, whatever is right, whatever is pure, whatever is lovely, whatever is admirable—if anything is excellent

or praiseworthy—think about such things."
(Philippians 4:8).

5. Rejecting Impurity
- To live according to God's commands, we need to reject lewdness and any form of immoral behavior. It's about making choices that align with God's will and promote a life of righteousness.

Scripture: "But among you there must not be even a hint of sexual immorality, or of any kind of impurity." (Ephesians 5:3).

In summary, biblical lewdness refers to behavior that is shameless, crude, or morally corrupt. It's about actions and attitudes that go against God's standards for purity and decency. The Bible encourages us to avoid lewdness and instead live in a way that reflects God's design for a pure and righteous life.

Uncleanness

In the Bible, uncleanness refers to a state of being morally or spiritually impure. It's about actions, thoughts, or conditions that go against God's standards of purity and righteousness.

Here's what you need to know.

1. Moral and Spiritual Impurity
- Uncleanness is when something or someone is considered impure or defiled according to God's standards. This can include sinful behavior, wrong thoughts, or anything that doesn't align with God's holiness.

Scripture: "For from within, out of the heart, come evil thoughts, sexual immorality, theft, murder, adultery, greed, malice, deceit, lewdness, envy, slander, arrogance and folly" (Mark 7:21-22).

2. Violation of God's Standards
- The Bible teaches that uncleanness involves actions or attitudes that violate God's commands. It's about living in a way that is contrary to what God has set as pure and acceptable.

Scripture: "Do not make yourselves unclean by any of these things, because this is how the nations that I am going to drive out before you became unclean" (Leviticus 18:24).

3. Impact on Relationship with God
- Being in a state of uncleanness affects your relationship with God. It can create a

barrier between you and Him, as He calls us to live in purity and holiness.

Scripture: "But your iniquities have separated you from your God; your sins have hidden his face from you, so that he will not hear." (Isaiah 59:2).

4. Call to Purity

- The Bible urges us to cleanse ourselves from all forms of uncleanness and live a life that reflects God's holiness. It's about rejecting sin and striving for a pure heart and mind.

Scripture: "Therefore, dear friends, since we have these promises, let us purify ourselves from everything that contaminates body and spirit, perfecting holiness out of reverence for God" (2 Corinthians 7:1).

5. Living in Righteousness

- To overcome uncleanness, we need to turn to God, confess our sins, and seek His forgiveness. It's about making choices that align with His commands and living a life that honors Him.

Scripture: "Create in me a pure heart, O God, and renew a steadfast spirit within me" (Psalm 51:10).

In summary, biblical uncleanness refers to moral or spiritual impurity, involving actions or attitudes that go against God's standards. The Bible encourages us to reject uncleanness, seek purity, and live in a way that aligns with God's holiness and righteousness.

Chapter 13

Morally Bad //
Shameful Things

The Greek word for bad is kakos, which means bad, evil. Usage of this word is bad and evil in the widest sense. Bad nature and not as it ought to be. According to the school of medicine, University of Missouri, morally wrong acts are activities such as murder, theft, rape, lying, and breaking promises. One of the ten commandments is not to murder. This commandment is against the law of the land here in America. Typically, you'll get a life sentence with no possibility of parole, death row while you wait to be executed, or 15 to life. It's also against the law to steal. It's against the law to physically harm anyone. In some states, it's still against the law to have sex with someone else's spouse. But most importantly, these acts are against the law of God.

Shameful things are things that make you feel bad, that you don't want to think about, things that you've done that you don't want anyone to know you've done. The secrets that you plan to keep until you die. Those are what are meant by shameful. Things such as watching pornography, paying for sex with prostitutes, having sex for money, being promiscuous, losing all your money gambling, fantasizing about being with married people, smoking, doing drugs, drinking too much, stealing, and attraction to the same sex. These things are detrimental because they cause guilt, and they are against God's way he wants us to live as Christians. These all stem from the fruits of the flesh. The flesh will never produce any good.

In the Bible, sexual immorality covers any kind of sexual behavior that goes against God's design and standards. It's a broad term that includes various forms of sinful sexual conduct.

Here's what you need to know:

1. Sexual Actions That Are Sinful

- Sexual immorality refers to any sexual activity that is considered sinful according to the Bible. This includes things like adultery, fornication, and other behaviors that deviate from God's plan for sex within marriage.

Scripture: "It is God's will that you should be sanctified: that you should avoid sexual immorality." (1 Thessalonians 4:3).

2. Violation of God's Design

- The Bible teaches that sex is meant to be enjoyed within the bounds of marriage between a man and a woman. Sexual immorality is anything outside of this design and is seen as a serious breach of God's standards.

Scripture: "Marriage should be honored by all, and the marriage bed kept pure, for God will judge the adulterer and all the sexually immoral." (Hebrews 13:4).

3. Impact on Spiritual Life

- Engaging in sexual immorality affects your relationship with God and can lead to spiritual and moral harm. It creates barriers between you and God, as it goes against His commands for purity.

Scripture: "Do you not know that wrongdoers will not inherit the kingdom of God? Do not be deceived: Neither the sexually immoral nor idolaters nor adulterers nor men who have sex with men." (1 Corinthians 6:9).

4. Call to Purity
- The Bible calls us to live in purity and avoid all forms of sexual immorality. This means following God's standards for sexuality and keeping our actions in line with His teachings.

Scripture: "Flee from sexual immorality. All other sins a person commits are outside the body, but whoever sins sexually, sins against their own body." (1 Corinthians 6:18).

5. Living According to God's Standards
- To overcome sexual immorality, you need to turn to God, seek His forgiveness, and strive to live in accordance with His design for sexuality. It's about making choices that honor Him and reflect His standards.

Scripture: "Create in me a pure heart, O God, and renew a steadfast spirit within me." (Psalm 51:10).

In summary, biblical sexual immorality refers to any sexual behavior that goes against

God's design and standards. It includes various forms of sinful conduct and is a serious breach of God's plan for sex, which is meant to be within marriage. The Bible encourages us to avoid sexual immorality and live in purity, aligning our actions with God's commands.

"No good tree bears bad fruit, nor does a bad tree bear good fruit. Each tree is recognized by its own fruit. People do not pick figs from thorn-bushes, or grapes from briers. A good man brings good things out of the good stored up in his heart, and an evil man brings evil things out of the evil stored up in his heart. For the mouth speaks what the heart is full of." Luke 6:43-45 NKJV

Chapter 14

Worship False Gods / Idols

What are false Gods [idols]? Anything we love more than we love God. Yours may not look the same as another. It is worshiping any other deity or religion that denies the true and living God. Anything or person you place your hope in more than God. It denies that Jesus is Lord. It diminishes Jesus Christ to just a good teacher and prophet. Some deny him existing at all. It also is the worship of the images of the biblical men and women. Including Mary, Paul, and Peter. What they did was great, but there is no reason to worship them. They were just vessels used by God who also had sin. But Jesus was the only one sinless who died on the cross for our sins. Jesus is also the only way that a man can get to the father God. Other things that can be a false God or an idol is yourself, beauty, material things, family, religion, careers, fame, attention, sex, science, money, drugs which includes weed that's a psychoactive drug from a cannabis plant, alcohol, comfort, education, gambling, power, entertainment, popularity, food, celebrities, and many more things.

Why are they detrimental?

1. Idolizing yourself will cause you to be selfish and make it impossible to love your neighbor as yourself. Idolizing yourself will make you prideful and make you think you're higher and better than everyone and that you don't need anyone. The bible says God resists the proud but gives grace to the humble. 1 Peter 5:5 NKJV The Greek word for resist is anthistémi meaning *take a complete stand against.* Do you want God to take a stand against you when you need him to answer your prayers and protect you? The Greek word for grace is Xaris is preeminently used of the Lord's *favor* – freely *extended to give Himself* away to people (because He is "always leaning

toward them"). Do you want the Lord's favor? You must be humble. If you are proud, remember our Lord has defeated death. Being against him is being against living. You will never have victory against or over God. He has defeated Satan, and he will defeat you.

2. Idolizing beauty will cause you to do things to alter the body God has given you to make it perfect in your small eyes. Things such as plastic surgery of any kind. Things like feeling like you cannot be seen without your hair and makeup done. Things like constantly posting pictures of yourself online and obsessing over all the likes and attention you get. The bible says Charm is deceitful and beauty is passing, but a woman who fears the Lord is worthy to be praised. Proverbs 31:30 NIV.

In the Bible, worshipping false gods and idols means giving reverence and devotion to things or beings that are not the one true God. This is seen as a serious offense because it turns your focus away from God and puts trust in things that cannot truly save or help. Here's what you need to know:

1. Reverence for Things Other Than God

- Worshipping false gods and idols means treating objects, images, or beings as if they are divine or worthy of worship. This could be anything from statues to imaginary deities that people believe can provide guidance or power.

Scripture: "You shall not make for yourself a graven image or any likeness of anything that is in heaven above or on the earth below or in the waters beneath the earth" (Exodus 20:4).

2. Turning Away from the True God

- When people worship false gods or idols, they are turning away from worshipping the true God. The Bible teaches that God is the only one deserving of our worship and devotion.

Scripture: "I am the Lord your God, who brought you out of Egypt, out of the land of slavery. You shall have no other gods before me" (Exodus 20:2-3).

3. Creating and Adoring Idols

- Idols are physical objects or images that people create to represent gods or spiritual beings. Worshipping these idols means giving them honor and reverence, which the Bible says should be reserved for God alone.

Scripture: "They have made for themselves a molten calf and have worshipped it, and have sacrificed to it and said, 'This is your god, O Israel, who brought you up from the land of Egypt!'" (Exodus 32:8).

4. Consequences of Idol Worship

- Worshipping false gods and idols leads to spiritual confusion and separation from God. It's seen as a form of disobedience that brings negative consequences and prevents true relationship with God.

Scripture: "Those who make them will be like them, and so will all who trust in them." (Psalm 115:8).

5. Call to Worship God Alone

- The Bible calls us to worship God alone and reject any form of idol worship. It's about directing our devotion and reverence solely to the one true God who created everything and deserves our complete loyalty.

Scripture: "Worship the Lord your God, and his blessing will be on your food and water.

I will take away sickness from among you" (Exodus 23:25).

In summary, biblical worship of false gods and idols refers to giving reverence to anything other than the one true God. It involves turning away from God and directing worship towards objects or beings that cannot save. The Bible emphasizes the importance of worshipping God alone and avoiding any form of idolatry.

Chapter 15

Witchcraft

Witchcraft- the practice of magic, especially for evil purposes, the use of spells.

3. Sorcery or magic

4. Communication with the devil or with a familiar (necromancy)

5. Rituals and practice that incorporate belief in magic and that are associated especially with neo-pagan traditions and religion. (Such as Wicca)

Define Witch: a specialist in the manipulation of the intangible power evils against people. Witches commonly held to have existed in the ancient Near East and were doubtless known to the ancient Israelites. The Old Testament contains lists of offenders of various kinds. The longest such list is found in Deut. 18:10-11, where the practitioners of various acts forbidden to the readers are said to flourish in the nations Israel is dispossessing. A slightly shorter list attributes such offenses to Manasseh. (2 Kings 21:6, 2 Chron 33:6), and several of the same terms are combined with the prophets and dreamers to whom Jeremiah tells the Judeans not to listen. (Jer. 27:9). Pairs of such terms are found in Lev. 19:26; Isa,. 47:9, 12 (Babylon); and Mic. 5:11. A woman who practices one of these activities and who may be a witch is proscribed in Exod. 22:18, and Nah. 3:4 designates Nineveh such a woman. The so-called witch of Endor (1 Sam. 28) is a necromancer or medium.

Practice of Wicca:

Use of tools- such as the broom (a purifying symbol), the wand, the candles, crystal, and the knife.

Synonyms of witchcraft:

1. Bewitchery: The power of bewitching or fascinating; charm.
2. Bewitchment: to affect by witchcraft or magic; cast a spell over.
3. Conjuring: To summon (a devil or spirit) by magical or supernatural power.

4. Devilry: black magic or other forms of diabolism.

5. Deviltry: reckless or unrestrained mischievous behavior. Extreme or utter wickedness.

6. Diablerie: diabolic magic or art; sorcery; witchcraft. The domain or realm of devils.

7. Enchantment: the state of being under a spell; magic.

8. Ensorcellment: The term typically refers to someone who has literally been put in a trance (as in fantasy stories) or to someone whose attention has been captured as if by magic (especially by a person they think is charming or beautiful).

9. Magic: the use of means (such as charms or spells) believed to have supernatural power over natural forces.

10. Mojo: a magic spell, hex, or charm.

11. Necromancy: of the spirits of the dead for purposes of magically revealing the future or influencing the course of events.

12.   Sorcery: the use of power gained from the assistance or control of evil spirits, especially for divining.

13.   Thaumaturgy: meaning "miracle working," is applicable to any performance of miracles, especially by incantation.(verbal rituals of magic)

14.   Voodism: a fusion of Afro-Caribbean Vodou and folk magic practiced chiefly in Louisiana, deriving ultimately from West African Vodun and containing elements borrowed from the Roman Catholic religion.

15.   Witchery: the practice of magic.

16.   Wizardry: the art or practice of magic.

You may have heard of black magic and white magic. Below are the definitions of them.

Black magic: magic involving the supposed of evil spirits for evil purposes.

White magic: **White magic** has traditionally referred to the use of supernatural powers or for selfless purposes. Practitioners of white magic have been given titles such as wise men or women, white witches or wizards. Many of these people claimed to have the ability to do such things because of knowledge or power that was passed on to them through hereditary lines, or by some event later in their lives. White magic was practiced through healing, blessing, charms, incantations, prayers, and songs. White magic is the benevolent counterpart of malicious.

White magic is considered good magic because it is used for what people consider good. However, as a bible believing Christian the Lord does not permit us to use any type of magic in the bible. In the bible it says that there is a way that *seems* RIGHT to man, but it ends is the way of death. Proverbs 14:12-16 NKJV.

It constantly says those who practice witchcraft will not inherit the kingdom of God.

Just like in Acts 19:17-20 may everyone who calls themselves a believer in the true and living God confess of what they have done. May they confess that they've used magic, done love spells, paid to have their tarot cards read, seen psychics, using sage, and throw away their new age spirituality books no matter how great the cause. May you repent and renounce all those evil things as your eyes and ears are becoming aware. May the veil be lifted from your eyes. May you confess that Jesus Christ is Lord and the only power that you need is the power of the HOLY SPIRIT! You have been warned!

In the Bible, worshipping false gods and idols means giving reverence and devotion to things or beings that are not the one true God. This is seen as a serious offense because it turns your focus away from God and puts trust in things that cannot truly save or help.

Here's what you need to know:

1. Reverence for Things Other Than God
   - Worshipping false gods and idols means treating objects, images, or beings as if they are divine or worthy of worship. This could be anything from statues to imaginary deities that people believe can provide guidance or power.
   Scripture: "You shall not make for yourself a graven image or any likeness of anything that is in heaven above or on the earth below or in the waters beneath the earth" (Exodus 20:4).

2. Turning Away from the True God
   - When people worship false gods or idols, they are turning away from worshipping the

true God. The Bible teaches that God is the only one deserving of our worship and devotion.

Scripture: "I am the Lord your God, who brought you out of Egypt, out of the land of slavery. You shall have no other gods before me" (Exodus 20:2-3).

3. Creating and Adoring Idols

- Idols are physical objects or images that people create to represent gods or spiritual beings. Worshipping these idols means giving them honor and reverence, which the Bible says should be reserved for God alone.

Scripture: "They have made for themselves a molten calf and have worshipped it, and have sacrificed to it and said, 'This is your god, O Israel, who brought you up from the land of Egypt!'" (Exodus 32:8).

4. Consequences of Idol Worship

- Worshipping false gods and idols leads to spiritual confusion and separation from God. It's seen as a form of disobedience that brings negative consequences and prevents true relationship with God.

Scripture: "Those who make them will be like them, and so will all who trust in them." (Psalm 115:8).

5. Call to Worship God Alone
- The Bible calls us to worship God alone and reject any form of idol worship. It's about directing our devotion and reverence solely to the one true God who created everything and deserves our complete loyalty.

Scripture: "Worship the Lord your God, and his blessing will be on your food and water. I will take away sickness from among you." (Exodus 23:25).

In summary, biblical worship of false gods and idols refers to giving reverence to anything other than the one true God. It involves turning away from God and directing worship towards objects or beings that cannot save. The Bible emphasizes the importance of worshipping God alone and avoiding any form of idolatry.

Chapter 16

Hatred / Trouble Starter / Causing Division

Hatred: extreme dislike or disgust: Ill will or resentment that is usually mutual: prejudice, hostility, or animosity.

"Whoever claims to love God yet hates a brother or sister is a liar. For whoever does not love their brother and sister, whom they have seen, cannot love God, whom they have not seen." 1 John 4:20 NIV.

We don't love because people are good, and they've done right by us. *"We love because he first loved us." 1 John 4:19 NIV.*

Love does not delight in evil but rejoices with the truth. 1 Corinthians 13:6 NIV.

What's a trouble starter? Someone who begins a fight causes a problem. This may be by their words, their attitude, their lack of respect or morals, their gossiping, backbiting, nosiness, meddling in people's business, etc. Consider the person who is always arguing, always fighting, and always falling out with people that they love. Think about the person who every time the go to a restaurant they are complaining and causing a scene.

Causing division is connected where you cause people or groups of people to hate each other for any reason. Instead of being a peacemaker, you draw a wedge between people.

Why is it detrimental?

Hating people stems from the lack of forgiveness, which will cause you to not be forgiven by God. You are disrupting the unity and harmony amongst people by starting trouble and causing division. It is also detrimental because it's toxic for your health, so much negativity, living tense, ready to war, and in survivor mode will eventually make you sick.

Chapter 17

Jealousy //

Enviousness

Jealousy- suspicious of a rival or one believed to enjoy an advantage.

Enviousness- painful or resentful awareness of another's advantages.

The perfect story to help you understand this is Saul and David's relationship.

David was Saul's servant. David started off playing the harp for Saul to chase the evil spirits away when they torment him. And then he defeated Goliath. Saul was impressed. He made David leader over the army, and he killed 10's of thousands. David was successful in any mission he was sent on. When he came from war, Saul heard the women singing songs and dancing saying Saul killed 1000s of people but David killed 10s of thousands. *"Saul was very angry; this refrain displeased him greatly. "They have credited David with tens of thousands," he thought, "but me with only thousands. What more can he get but the kingdom?" And from that time on Saul kept a close eye on David." 1 Samuel 18:8-9 NIV* Saul's jealousy causes him to chase David and become delusional, thinking that David was against him and wanted to kill him. Saul was caught by David while he was pursuing him, and David had mercy on him and did not kill him, even though he kept trying to kill him. David honored Saul as God's appointed king. But Saul lost everything due to his own disobedience to God. David was chosen to be next as the King of Israel by God. The complete story is found in 1 Samuel 18. The next day, an evil spirit came over Saul and he took a spear and threw it full force, trying to pin David to the wall twice!

Chapter 18

Being Drunk // Wild Parties

Why they're detrimental?

When you go to wild parties, you do things you wouldn't ordinarily do if you weren't at a wild party. At these parties literally anything goes. It's an open door to engage in all kinds of sin. Wild parties you show an extreme lack of restraint and control. It does not produce any good fruit. It gives birth to you, doing more and more things that you wouldn't ordinarily do. So, you may go from screaming and jumping on the table, to popping pills people give you, to kissing some random person, to dancing more and more provocatively. These things lead to you getting sick the next day with headaches and stomachaches. A lot of people are throwing up everywhere. Do you not realize that is not the fruit of a good time? You're putting your life in danger and purposely making yourself sick. Some people get so drunk they even must go to the hospital to get their stomach pumped and IV fluids in their body because they are so dehydrated. Being drunk and high alters your state of mind. Being drunk and high only numbs you for a moment. Wild parties, being high, and drinking will not remove all your worries. You numb them for the night and remember them when you sober up. There is another way to freedom that is not just temporary. That freedom is through accepting Jesus as your Lord and savior. He can heal you and deliver you from every pain, trail, tribulation, betrayal, hurt, and heartbreak you may feel. Many have experienced the same heartbreaks because of sin such as rape, abuse, being cheating on, lied to, stolen from, and people we love dying before we were ready for them too. You are not the only one who has experienced the pain that hurt you so bad. Some of us have instead of running to numbing devices (i.e., smoking, drinking, sex, partying) we ran to the great physician Jesus and allowed him to heal us. Allowed him to do the operation on us so we can look like and feel like we've never been broken before. The heart that broke when we were betrayed over and over, God can mend our heart back together again. We can be able to love like we have never been hurt. We can live in the freedom like someone who has never been hurt by choosing to forgive and let it go. Those heinous betrayals we experienced want to victimize us forever and retraumatize us every single time we think about what happened to us. Those experiences want to steal your identity from whoever you are and rename you VICTIM. What is a victim? A person harmed, injured, or killed as a result of a crime, accident, or other event or action. Another definition is a person who is tricked or duped. But if you are reading this, you are a SURVIVOR! What's a survivor? A person who survives, especially a person remaining alive after an event in which others have died. But today I rename you, if you are reading this book, I declare and decree you are indeed an OVERCOMER in the mighty name of Jesus! What is an OVERCOMER? A person who overcomes something: one who succeeds in dealing with or gaining control of some problem or difficulty. But it is Jesus Christ who will help you remain an OVERCOMER. Stay in his word, in his presence, and in prayer. Every single day a thought, song, word, movie, show or experience may trigger you and you may want to go back to being a victim because it feels familiar. But I charge you to rise up and remember that if you are one of God's children, he that is in you is stronger than he that is in the world! That which hurt you is of the past. It can't hurt you anymore, it can't control you anymore, it can't torment you anymore, the power it had over you is gone. Forgive the people that hurt you as an act of your will and watch the freedom you receive. If they are ex's and ex friends forgive them but don't give them access into your life to allow them to victimize you again. But if it's your spouse, children, parents, and good friends that have your best interest at heart, forgive but set boundaries. Be upfront and honest about how they hurt you and how you want to be treated going forward. Listen to how you hurt them and how they want to be treated as well. A relationship with anyone is a compromise and a two-way street. We can't set expectations that are unknown. We must make them clear and accept their expectations as well.

ShaRhonda D. Williams147

You are

worth

dying for

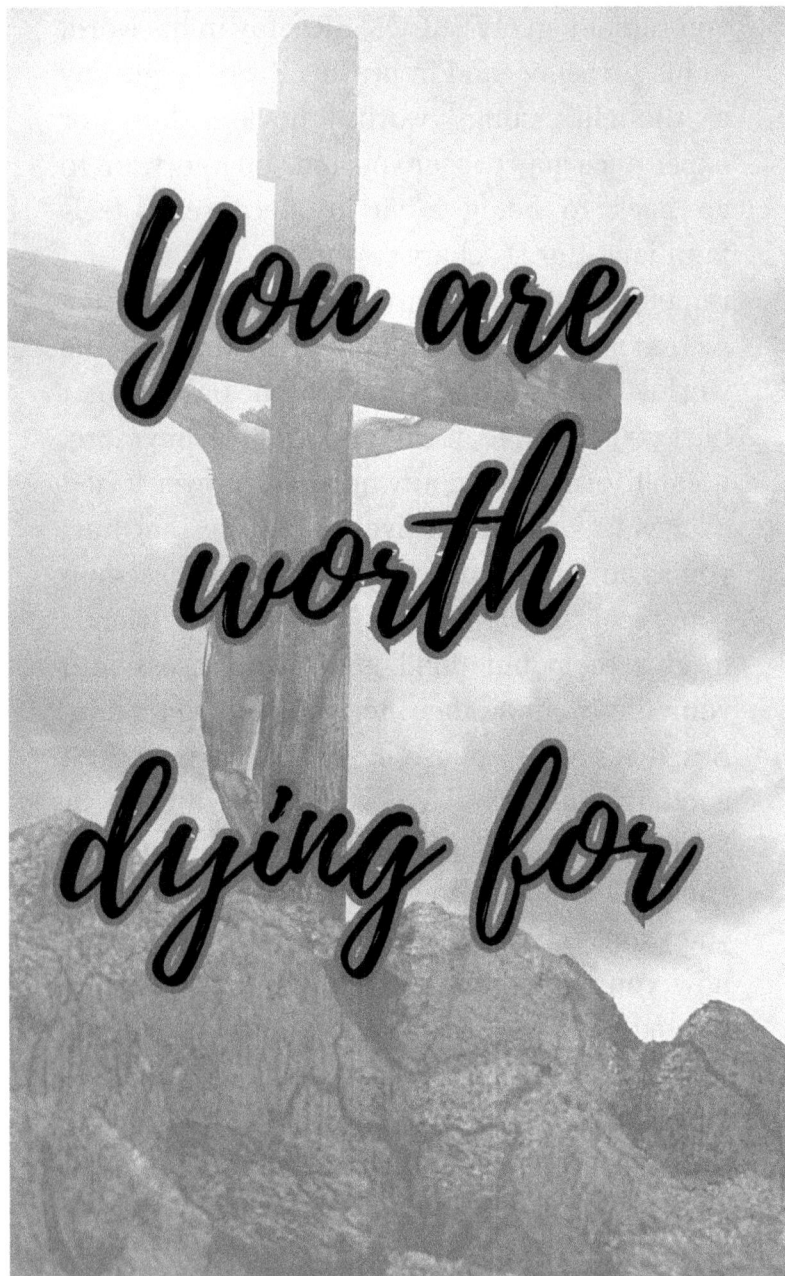

ShaRhonda D. Williams 148

Chapter 19

You are

Worth Dying

For

Consider this: If you only think about the pleasures and desires of today, then it will make all of this seem not so bad. Jesus thought of us thousands of years before we would ever be born. He had love, peace, joy, gifts, talents, forgiveness, and blessings waiting for us. Your eyes, being able to read this book, are a blessing from God. My hands typing on this page is a blessing from God. Us being in our right mind is a blessing from God. When you consider the blessings or the curses your decisions have on your family, please take heed. I know it's easiest understood in financial terms. So, here's an example: if a man invests his money well as a young man when he dies, his sons and daughters can still benefit from that. If a man invests his money foolishly or is selfish, his children will suffer when he dies. Think the same with your choices. God's word says, *"Therefore know that the LORD your God, He is God, the faithful God who keeps covenant and mercy for a thousand generations with those who love Him and keep His commandments; and He repays those who hate Him to their face to destroy them. He will not be slack with him who hates Him; He will repay him to his face." Deuteronomy 7:9 NKJV* We are not the only ones affected by our choices. Our spouses, children, siblings, families, friends, and strangers are affected as well. A lot of the things we do others follow it, rather they tell us they are or not. Our life is not merely made up of us doing whatever pleases our flesh. But it has such a greater value than just that. Our lives speak to others, our lives influence others, our life empowers others, and encouragers others. However, you only can influence people to be holy or unholy. When we teach young people to have safe sex instead of unprotected sex, that is good, right? Wrong! Instead, we should teach them purity and the beauty of protecting the vessel God gave them and not polluting it with sex partners that are not your spouse. Safe sex isn't safe if it still leads to sexually immorality, soul ties, emotional soul ties, toxic relationship, domestic violence, pregnancy scares, abortions, plan b pills, broken hearts, and impurity. I know you may be thinking well it's better for them not to have babies outside of wedlock and std's. I beg to differ because some people learn the hard way and those things happening to them either make them reevaluate themselves and surrender to Christ or fool themselves by thinking they can be safer in sexual immorality. It is the safest to not indulge in sexual immorality. God's original design for things is for our protection. He's not merely trying to take away your fun. Seeing as he can see the heart and how you leave fragments of yourself with every person you have sex with. Broken people sleep around because they want to feel validated, loved, and wanted. They are lost and don't know who they are. If you were secure in who you were, you would realize you are valuable and no human that God created can give you value. Why? Because your value was set on the cross when Christ died for your sins. Your value = **WORTH DYING FOR**, even though you're guilty. God knew you would be a sinner, liar, backslider, fornicator, confused, lost, disobedient. But instead of us having to make atonement (payment) for our sin by slaying innocent animals, God sent his son Jesus, to be the atonement for our sin once and for all. Now it has been made easy for us. We get to choose to believe in Jesus and accept him as our Lord and Savior. We get to choose to repent, which means to turn away from our wicked ways. We get to choose to be baptized. We get to choose to be filled with the holy ghost with evidence of speaking in tongues. Our lack of fear and reverence for God is the driving force behind walking in the flesh instead of walking in the spirit. I believe that's why God had this book written for you to better understand the what the fruits of the spirit are and what the fruit of the flesh are. I will insert in more resources for you to continue your study on these matters. Please take heed that books like these are for mercy so that you can know so that you can repent while you still have time. Remember that you are responsible for the choices that you make, no matter who told you to do them. Walking in the flesh will steal your peace. But if you walk in the flesh and deny your flesh, you can experience true peace. God Bless.

Chapter 20

Repentance

The key to sustaining your deliverance and maintaining your peace lies in embracing a lifestyle of repentance. Rooted in the Greek word "metanoia," meaning a change of mind and repentance, this daily practice ensures ongoing spiritual renewal and alignment with God's will.

I want you to understand that you are not too far gone, too dirty, too bad. You are loved. You are created in the image of God. Just like the prodigal son, our Lord would embrace you with open arms when you repent and come return to your first love. If you have indulged and over-indulged in every kind of fruit of the flesh and broken every commandment you can still be forgiven. The key is to repent before it's too late. When is it too late? The day that you're dead and no longer able to ask for forgiveness. So everyday is a great day to confess your sins to

God. Tell him everything, he knows everything. But your confession is you taking accountability for your actions. Our God is just to forgive you if you ask. He died so we'd be forgiven and because he loves us so much.

Repentance is not a one-time event but a continuous process. Each day presents opportunities for growth and self-reflection, and it's essential to acknowledge and repent for any sins, regardless of their perceived magnitude. No sin is insignificant, and maintaining a clear conscience before God requires consistent repentance.

Scripture emphasizes the importance of repentance as a pathway to righteousness. When confronted with our sins, we are called to repent and renounce them without delay, aligning our hearts with God's divine will. Ignoring or delaying repentance only serves to distance us from His grace and love. In this guide, you'll find scriptural references affirming the call to repentance and a self-deliverance framework to aid you on your journey towards spiritual wholeness. By embracing a lifestyle of repentance and self-reflection, you'll cultivate a deeper connection with God and experience lasting peace and fulfillment.

ShaRhonda D. Williams155

Chapter 21

Self

Deliverance

Every day is a good practice to go through self-deliverance. Living a lifestyle of repentance, obedience to the word of God, and forgiveness will keep you free. Instead of being a slave to sin, the bible says to offer ourselves to be a slave to righteousness leading to holiness. Romans 6:15-23 Pray and ask the Lord to bring down his deliverance angels to help deliver you.

I repent for (state your sin aloud) in the name of Jesus.

I come out of agreement with (state your sin aloud) in the name of Jesus.

I break covenant with (state your sin aloud) in the name of Jesus.

I renounce (state your sin aloud) in the name of Jesus.

I denounce (state your sin aloud) in the name of Jesus.

Pray that God send his deliverance angels to fully deliver you from anything you are bound to, any chains you are chained to, remove blinders from your eyes, remove plugs out of your ears. Ask God to forgive you and heal you. Ask God to humble you so that you will learn to trust him completely. Ask God to renew a right spirit in you and a clean heart. Ask God to bring to your mind everything you need to repent, renounce, and come out of agreement with. Ask God to show you who you need to forgive and help you to forgive them with your whole heart.

Renounce pride every day. The bible says he resists the proud and gives grace to the humble.' James 4:6 NKJV

None of us can afford for God to resist our prayers. We cannot. That means you walk around and have no protection from God. We need God's protection. So, every day come out of agreement with pride and renounce it daily! Recommit yourself to our Lord and Savior

Jesus. Every day you feel led allow the Lord to show you what areas of your life you need to pray for him to change, heal, and soften.

1. Matthew 3:2

Repent, for the kingdom of heaven is at hand.

2. Matthew 3:8

Bear fruit in keeping with repentance.

3. Matthew 3:11

I baptize you with water for repentance, but he who is coming after me is mightier than I, whose sandals I am not worthy to carry. He will baptize you with the Holy Spirit and fire.

4. Matthew 4:17

From that time Jesus began to preach, saying, "Repent, for the kingdom of heaven is at hand."

5. Matthew 11:20-21

Then he began to denounce the cities where most of his mighty works had been done, because they did not repent. "Woe to you, Chorazin! Woe to you, Bethsaida! For if the mighty works done in you had been done in Tyre and Sidon, they would have repented long ago in sackcloth and ashes."

6. Matthew 12:41 The men of Nineveh will rise at the judgment with this generation and

condemn it, for they repented at the preaching of Jonah, and behold, something greater than Jonah is here.

7. Matthew 1:15

"The time is fulfilled, and the kingdom of God is at hand; repent and believe in the gospel."

8. Mark 1:4

John appeared, baptizing in the wilderness and proclaiming a baptism of repentance for the forgiveness of sins.

9. Mark 6:12

So, they went out and proclaimed that people should repent.

10. Luke 3:3

And he went into all the region around the Jordan, proclaiming a baptism of repentance for the forgiveness of sins.

11. Luke 3:8

Bear fruits in keeping with repentance. And do not begin to say to yourselves, "We have Abraham as our father. For I tell you, God is able from these stones to raise up children for Abraham.

12. Luke 5:32

I have not come to call the righteous but sinners to repentance.

13. Luke 13:3

No, I tell you; but unless you repent, you will all likewise perish.

14. Luke 15:7

Just so, I tell you, there will be more joy in heaven over one sinner who repents than over ninety-nine persons who need no repentance.

15. Luke 15:10

Just so, I tell you, there is joy before the angels of God over one sinner who repents.

16. Luke 17:3

Pay attention to yourselves! If your brother sins, rebuke him, and if he repents, forgive him.

17. Acts 2:38

And Peter said to them, "Repent and be baptized every one of you in the name of Jesus Christ for the forgiveness of your sins, and you will receive the gift of the Holy Spirit."

18. Acts 3:19

Repent therefore, and turn back, that your sins may be blotted out.

19. Acts 8:22

Repent, therefore, of this wickedness of yours, and pray to the Lord that, if possible, the intent of your heart may be forgiven you.

20. Acts 11:18

When they heard these things, they fell silent. And they glorified God, saying, "Then to the Gentiles also God has granted repentance that leads to life."

21. Romans 2:4

Or do you presume on the riches of his kindness and forbearance and patience, not knowing that God's kindness is meant to lead you to repentance?

Chapter 22

The Vitality

of Forgiveness

The scriptures remind us that some battles cannot be won without prayer and fasting. Begin with your parents. The Bible instructs us to honor our father and mother, a commandment accompanied by a promise: that it may be well with us and that we may enjoy long life on the earth (Ephesians 6:1-4, NIV; Exodus 20:12). Our parents are often the longest-lasting figures in our lives, present before we have the choice to embrace or reject them. This proximity can lead to profound wounds; they may have disappointed or hurt us deeply. However, if we trace our capacity for forgiveness back to those first connections and extend it to our parents, we can learn to forgive anyone.

Holding onto unforgiveness toward our parents for years can take root in our souls. Examine your life: Are you battling any unexplained illnesses? Are doctors unable to pinpoint their origin, or attributing them to hereditary issues? There's a connection. Unforgiveness can manifest as sickness, often passed down through generations, wreaking havoc on our bloodlines. Just as the consequences of sin extend from Adam and Eve, our grudges can echo through our families, affecting future generations. Consider the weight of your unforgiveness—what impact will it have on your children and loved ones?

Freedom is available through Christ, who forgives us no matter our past, provided we repent. Forgive your parents, understanding that they acted out of ignorance. Some wounds cut deeper than others, yet they still ache. Ask God to assist you in forgiving wholeheartedly, so you may be healed and restored. Many find it difficult to forgive those they love deeply, expecting loyalty in return. Reflect on the immense love of Jesus, who endured a criminal's death for you, fully aware of your betrayals. He still chose to extend forgiveness, offering you a chance for redemption.

Few parents would endure the torment Christ faced for their children. We often overlook how blessed we are by the profound love shown to us. It is humbling to think someone would bear the weight of our sins so we could be forgiven. Even when we are wronged, God stands as our advocate, loving us despite our guilt. He is both our judge and our defender, providing us the means to confess, repent, and renew ourselves. He is a good Father and our Redeemer; we were lost, and now we are found. God, we worship Your holy name.

I urge you to forgive your siblings, family, and friends. The Bible is clear: if we do not forgive, we will not be forgiven (Matthew 6:14-15). You may question if a particular offense is too great to forgive or if there is a limit to how many times we should overlook transgressions. Under heaven, no offense is beyond forgiveness, and we should not impose numerical limits. Scripture advises us to forgive "seventy times seven" times—technically 490 times—but we should aim never to reach that number. True forgiveness wipes the slate clean, allowing each new hurt to be treated as if it were the first.

ShaRhonda D. Williams | 64

Exercise wisdom in choosing who to keep close. Ask God for clarity when someone causes you pain. Is this a situation where you are called to endure, or is it one where you should forgive and separate for your well-being? Relationships with spouses, parents, children, and cherished friends are invaluable, yet seasons change, and the Word of God remains eternal. If a relationship is seasonal and becomes destructive, seek God's will through prayer and fasting to discern if reconciliation is possible. If not, do not look back; heed His guidance and follow it, for we face enough heartbreak without compounding it through disobedience.

When you are hurt or betrayed, bring your pain to God swiftly. Be honest in your prayers; share your story in detail as you would with a trusted friend. Listen for His response. If you seek understanding, ask why this happened. But don't forget to ask for His help in forgiving those who wronged you. Consider writing a letter detailing their actions and your feelings, then declare aloud: "I release [name] into my forgiveness for [what they did and how it affected me] in the name of Jesus Christ." If anger or revenge rises within you, consider fasting. Some burdens cannot be lifted without dedicated prayer and fasting.

Reject everyday unforgiveness; you do not want God to turn away your prayers. Surrender the right to harbor resentment or self-pity, for pride can trap you in these dark places. Remember, holding onto your rights may lead you to be unforgiven by God, who has every right against us. If God resists the proud, understand that refusing to humble yourself keeps you outside His will and protection, leaving you vulnerable to the enemy's attacks.

Satan eagerly seeks open doors to infiltrate our lives, just as those desperate for food flock to free meals. He is relentless in his desire to kill, steal, and destroy God's people—those who believe in Jesus and His sacrifice. Just as soldiers become targets of those who oppose their country, we, as God's children, become enemies of the adversary. Let us remain vigilant, knowing that while he seeks our downfall, God has already secured our victory through Christ.

Word of The Lord

Many are the prayers of the righteous, but few will be answered because you are unforgiving. You have to come back to the basics and forgive everyone who has offended you, hurt you, lied to you, and betrayed you. It cannot stay in you, it must die. Forgive for your freedom. Forgive because your life is dependent on it. The diseases that unforgiveness cause are treacherous and aggressive. The cure to them is forgiveness. Start with yourself. And every time I bring to your memory someone you need to forgive release them into your forgiveness quickly as an act of your will. Repent and renounce holding onto unforgiveness. The more you hold onto it the more calamity will hold on to you. It is freedom in forgiveness. For your mind, body, and soul. This is another gift that you're freely given, so you need to freely give it.

ShaRhonda D. Williams167

Let it go and let it go now. Stop reasoning with sin. Your refusal to forgive is sin, and it is disgusting in my eyes after I died, so you could be forgiven. It doesn't matter what they did or what they said. Forgive them anyway. You get to choose every day who you'll wake up and serve. Walking in unforgiveness is walking in the flesh because lingering unforgiveness turns to hate. How could you hate your brother but love me, who you've never seen? I created them too, and I died for them too. Forgive child forgive.

Chapter 23

Forgiveness

Mandate

As a Christian, the Bible must serve as your ultimate authority. This means that regardless of your emotions, upbringing, or personal beliefs, when you discover that your values, morals, and thoughts conflict with scripture, it is your responsibility to align them with the Word of God. Each time you grow in your understanding of God and His principles, you must commit to obeying them. We are called to study the scriptures diligently to show ourselves approved.

If your feelings dictate your actions, you will find yourself in peril. Emotions can be danger.

One moment, anger may urge you to react—perhaps to confront someone who disrespected you. The next, it might lead you to indulge in that extra donut. Such fickle feelings are unreliable; they come and go. It's essential to assess your feelings and categorize your thoughts. If any thought contradicts the Word of God, you must set aside your emotions to obey scripture rather than giving into your flesh.

Now, let's explore what the scripture teaches us about forgiveness.

The Parable of the Unforgiving Servant

Matthew 18:21-35

Then Peter came to Jesus and asked, "Lord, when someone won't stop doing wrong to me, how many times must I forgive them? Seven times?" Jesus answered, "I tell you, you must forgive them more than seven times. You must continue to forgive them even if they do wrong to you seventy-seven times. "So God's kingdom is like a king who decided to collect the money his servants owed him. The king began to collect his money. One servant owed him several thousand pounds of silver. He was not able to pay the money to his master, the king. So the master ordered that he and everything he owned be sold, even his wife and children. The money would be used to pay the king what the servant owed. "But the servant fell on his knees and begged, 'Be patient with me. I will pay you everything I owe.' The master felt sorry for him. So he told the servant he did not have to pay. He let him go free. "Later, that same servant found another servant who owed him a hundred silver coins. He grabbed him around the neck and said, 'Pay me the money you owe me!' "The other servant fell on his knees and begged him, 'Be patient with me. I will pay you everything I owe.' "But the first servant refused to be patient. He told the judge that the other servant owed him money, and that servant was put in jail until he could pay everything he owed. All the other servants saw what happened. They felt very sorry for the man. So they went and told their master everything that happened. "Then the master called his servant in and said, 'You evil servant. You begged me to forgive your debt, and I said you did not have to pay anything! So you should have given that other man who serves with you the same mercy I gave you.' The master was very angry, so he put the servant in jail to be punished. And he had to stay in jail until he could pay everything he owed. "This king did the same as my heavenly Father will do to you. You must forgive your brother or sister with all your heart, or my heavenly Father will not forgive you."

This story concludes with a powerful reminder: if we fail to forgive from the depths of our hearts, we risk facing a fate like that of the unforgiving servant in the parable. Just as the king dealt with that servant, so too will God respond to us. It's crucial to understand that if we must bear the penalty for our sins, it ultimately means facing death and spending eternity separated from God. Forgiveness is not just a choice; it's a vital aspect of our spiritual journey.

Luke 11:4

"And forgive us our sins; for we also forgive every one that is indebted to us. And lead us not into temptation; but deliver us from evil." KJV

Matthew 6:14

"For if ye forgive men their trespasses, your heavenly Father will also forgive you." KJV

Matthew 6:15

"But if ye forgive not men their trespasses, neither will your Father forgive your trespasses." KJV

Ephesians 1:7
"In whom we have redemption through his blood, the forgiveness of sins, according to the riches of his grace;" KJV

Matthew 6:14 (ESV)
For if you forgive others their trespasses, your heavenly Father will also forgive you,

Matthew 6:15
But if you refuse to forgive others, your Father will not forgive your sins.

Ephesians 1:7 (ESV)
In him we have redemption through his blood, the forgiveness of our trespasses, according to the riches of his grace,

Acts 10:43 (ESV)
To him all the prophets bear witness that everyone who believes in him receives forgiveness of sins through his name."

<u>1 John 1:9</u>

If we confess our sins, he is faithful and just and will forgive us our sins and purify us from all unrighteousness.

<u>Mark 11:25 (ESV)</u>

And whenever you stand praying, forgive, if you have anything against anyone, so that your Father also who is in heaven may forgive you your trespasses."

Chapter 24

Ending

Prayer

May every word contained within these pages serve as a source of blessing and inspiration to you. May the Lord's abundant blessings encompass you, safeguarding you with His love and grace. May your heart overflow with peace, joy, strength, and courage, empowering you to navigate life's challenges with resilience and boldness.

May every spiritual chain that binds you be shattered in the mighty name of Jesus. May the veil of darkness be lifted from your eyes, allowing you to see the light of God's truth clearly. Let every fear be dispelled from your mind, and may your heart be liberated from all bondage.

As the scriptures declare, "blessed are your eyes, for they see, and your ears, for they hear." (Matthew 13:16 KJV) May you be granted discernment and understanding, enabling you to perceive the wonders of God's kingdom.

May you be delivered from every tormenting spirit, finding solace and refuge in the arms of the true and living God. Surrender yourself wholeheartedly to His divine will, walking in unwavering obedience and experiencing the fullness of His blessings in Jesus' name. Amen.

Resources

1. Before you try anything else **THE BIBLE.** The bible must be your final authority above feelings and any and all other voices. "All scripture is God-breathed and is useful for teaching, rebuking, correcting, and training in righteousness that the servant of God may be thoroughly equipped for every good work." 2 Timothy 3:16-17

The bible is infallible.

Cross reference the King James Version with other versions of the bible to help you understand it. Easy read version of the bible is great. New King James version is great. English Standard Version is great. Amplified Version is great.

2. You version Bible App is great. Many translations on the app to help you cross-reference

which just means looking at a few different translations at once to better understand. It is an app on your phone. It also has bible studies that are called Plans. The have many plans for new believers, women, men, husbands, wives, mothers, fathers, lost, hopeless, read the bible in a year challenge, read the bible in 3 months challenge, daily scripture. A feature where you can type in how you feel to see what the bible says. Feelings such as love, anxiety, fear, anger, and much more.

Download from the app store.

3. Bible Gateway | Cross reference scriptures on screen at same time. Good when using computers also works on phones.

4. Bible Hub for translation of words in scripture. The Old Testament was originally written in Hebrew and the New Testament was originally written in Greek.

5. Thomas Nelson Women's Bible Studies | My favorite is the NKJV second edition Similar one is linked.

6. Old school Bible Concordances & Dictionaries

7. DREAM INTERPRETATIONS [GOD ONLY] – Google sends you to new age websites, people give you their own interpretations, so please do yourself a favor and ask God what did the dream mean?

Daily Dream Prayer

Father if this dream is of You then I come into agreement with it according to Jeremiah 29:11 because You said that Your thoughts towards me were of good and not of evil to give me an expected end. So based on that scripture, whatever You're revealing to me is for my benefit and I bind myself to it. If this dream is NOT from You, if the enemy has caused me to come into agreement with something that's detrimental to my life - I reject it, renounce it, denounce myself from every evil covenant in that dream! I see where the enemy is trying to

ShaRhanda D. Williams181

block me again, but now that I came to this understanding, I break every evil covenant and every evil sacrifice and every evil voice speaking to my destiny. Father, just like you hailed down fire and brimstone from Sodom and Gomorrah, rain down spiritual fire and brimstone against every evil act against my life. Whatever is hindering me, whatever is delaying me, pull up every spiritual demonic anchor that has anchored me to a place of non-progress - in the mighty name of Jesus Christ!!!" (Prayer from Minister Kevin Ewing during the Art of War message)

8.W A R N I N G: Any book recommended please read alongside your bible. Pray before you read it. If you don't feel led to read them don't. The bible is the most important tool in life. Many beautiful illustrations and examples of how to live a Christian life in right standing with God. Those books below are written by imperfect humans and by no way am I saying I agree with every single thing they have written in these books I recommend. Some things have been helpful and some I do not agree with. Use your bible and the guidance of the holy spirit to see if the books below or any books line up, go against the bible, are extra biblical revelations, or just mere opinions/suggestions. God bless you and continuously put on the full armor of God.

Books on DELIVERANCE:

9. **Setting Captives Free Deliverance Manual by Bev Tucker**

10. **Deliverance from Demonic Covenants and Curses by Rev. Joseph A. Solomon [Amazon only]**

https://www.amazon.com/Deliverance-Demonic-Covenants-Curses-Solomon/dp/1609573382/ref=sr_1_1?crid=38QTTL5KTXNVZ&keywords=deliverance+from+demonic+covenants+and+curses+workbook&qid=1693942473&s=books&sprefix=delivera%2Cstripbooks%2C135&sr=1-1

Books on prayer and holiness

11. **Destroying Fear | Strategies to Overthrow The Enemy's Tactic And Walk In Total Freedom by John Ramirez** [everywhere books are sold] https://www.amazon.com/Destroying-Fear-Strategies-Overthrow-Tactics/dp/080079947X/ref=sr_1_1?crid=1LRG1ZCUWRAZK&keywords=fear+john+ramirez&qid=1693942392&s=books&sprefi

x=fear+john+ramirez%2Cstripb
ooks%2C116&sr=1-1

12.   **Armed   &
Dangerous By John Ramirez**
https://www.amazon.com/Arme
d-Dangerous-Ultimate-
Targeting-
Defeating/dp/0800798503/ref=
sr_1_4?crid=3TRYBWH53N3P0
&keywords=john+ramirez&qid=
1693942847&s=books&sprefix=j
ohn+ramirez%2Cstripbooks%2C
115&sr=1-4

13.   **Fervent   Prayer
Priscilla Shirer** [she explains
how the enemy comes through to
destroy different areas of your
life.
https://www.amazon.com/Fervent-
Womans-Serious-Specific-
Strategic/dp/1433688670/ref=sr_1_1?crid=O
A5M9VHUU9JJ&keywords=fervent+book+pri
scilla+shirer&qid=1693942338&s=books&spre
fix=ferverent+%2Cstripbooks%2C132&sr=1-1

14.   **Pursuit   of
Holiness by Jerry Bridges**
https://www.amazon.com/Pursu

it-Holiness-Jerry-
Bridges/dp/1631466399

15. The Power Of A Praying Wife

https://www.amazon.com/Power-
Praying®-Wife-Book-
Prayers/dp/0736957510/ref=sr_1_2_sspa?cri
d=14KR814ZQN8IM&keywords=prayers+wife
&qid=1702059704&s=books&sprefix=prayers+
wife%2Cstripbooks%2C141&sr=1-2-
spons&sp_csd=d2lkZ2VoTmFtZT1zcF9hdGY&
psc=1

16. What he Must Be by Voddie Bacham Jr.

https://www.amazon.com/What-He-Must-
Be-
Daughter/dp/1581349300/ref=asc_df_158134
9300/?tag=hyprod-
20&linkCode=df0&hvadid=312034012759&hv
pos=&hvnetw=g&hvrand=1099797455025046
3527&hvpone=&hvptwo=&hvqmt=&hvdev=c&
hvdvcmdl=&hvlocint=&hvlocphy=9027812&hv
targid=pla-563374626866&psc=1

17. Family Worship by Voddie Bacham Jr.

Daughters/dp/1433528126/ref=sr_1_1?cri
d=UCHNTQSS7SN3&keywords=family+driven

+faith&qid=1702059330&s=books&sprefix=fa
mily+driven+%2Cstripbooks%2C138&sr=1-1

18. **Kingdom
Woman by Tony Evans and
daughter Chrystal Evans
Hurst**

https://www.amazon.com/Kingdom-
Woman-Embracing-Purpose-
Possibilities/dp/1624053548/ref=sr_1_1?crid
=31CNWHMWD4XYW&keywords=kingdom+
woman&qid=1695236652&s=books&sprefix=k
ingdom+woman%2Cstripbooks%2C128&sr=1-1

19. **Kingdom Man by
Tony Evans**

https://www.amazon.com/Kingdom-Man-
Every-Destiny-
Womans/dp/1589977475/ref=sr_1_1?crid=2M
7ZF95ALZ421&keywords=kingdom+man&qid
=1695236699&s=books&sprefix=kingdom+ma
n+%2Cstripbooks%2C121&sr=1-1

20. **Kingdom
Marriage by Tony Evans**

https://www.amazon.com/Kingdom-
Marriage-Connecting-Purpose-
Pleasure/dp/1589978900/ref=sr_1_1_sspa?cri
d=2JQ1MILK2ZWBK&keywords=kingdom+m
arriage&qid=1695236770&s=books&sprefix=ki

ngdom+marriage%2Cstripbooks%2C143&sr=1-
1-
spons&sp_csd=d2lkZ2V0TmFtZT1zcF9hdGY&
psc=1

Peace, in your mind, body, and soul

Citation's

ShaRhonda D. Williams187

Peace, in your mind, body, and soul

Sinners Prayer

"HAVE MERCY ON ME, O
GOD,ACCORDING TO YOUR UNFAILING
LOVE;ACCORDING TO YOUR GREAT
COMPASSION BLOT OUT MY
TRANSGRESSIONS.WASH AWAY ALL
MY INIQUITY AND CLEANSE ME FROM
MY SIN.FOR I KNOW MY
TRANSGRESSIONS,AND MY SIN IS
ALWAYS BEFORE ME.AGAINST YOU,
YOU ONLY, HAVE I SINNED AND DONE
WHAT IS EVIL IN YOUR SIGHT,SO THAT
YOU ARE PROVED RIGHT WHEN YOU
SPEAK AND JUSTIFIED WHEN YOU
JUDGE.SURELY I HAVE BEEN A SINNER
FROM BIRTH,SINFUL FROM THE TIME
MY MOTHER CONCEIVED ME...
CLEANSE ME WITH HYSSOP, AND I
WILL BE CLEAN;WASH ME AND I WILL
BE WHITER THAN SNOW...CREATE IN
ME A PURE HEART, O GOD,AND RENEW
A STEADFAST SPIRIT WITHIN ME.DO
NOT CAST ME FROM YOUR PRESENCE
OR TAKE YOUR HOLY SPIRIT FROM
ME.RESTORE TO ME THE JOY OF YOUR
SALVATION AND GRANT ME A WILLING
SPIRIT TO SUSTAIN ME.THEN WILL I
TEACH TRANSGRESSORS YOUR
WAYS,AND SINNERS WILL TURN BACK
TO YOU."

Psalm 51 NIV

ShaRhonda D. Williams188

About The Author

ShaRhonda D. Williams is a beacon of hope and a testament to the transformative power of God's love and grace. As an author, speaker, and advocate for spiritual healing and restoration, ShaRhonda shares her journey of overcoming adversity with unwavering faith and resilience.

Born and raised in a tumultuous environment, ShaRhonda experienced firsthand the devastating effects of domestic violence, trauma, and sin. However, her life took a dramatic turn when she encountered the redeeming love of Jesus Christ. Through His grace, ShaRhonda found the strength to break free from the chains of her past and embrace a life of purpose and fulfillment.

ShaRhonda's writings reflect her deep-rooted commitment to spreading the message of hope, forgiveness, and spiritual renewal. Her candid memoirs and insightful teachings inspire others to confront their own struggles and seek healing through faith and repentance.

With a heart full of compassion and a desire to see lives transformed, ShaRhonda continues to share her story with audiences around the world. Through her books, speaking engagements, and online platforms, she empowers individuals to embrace the freedom and peace that can only be found in Christ.

ShaRhonda resides in the great state of Texas, where she enjoys spending time with her family, homeschooling, homemaking, blogging, and spreading the message of God's unfailing love.

Stay Connected:

Request to speak or be interviewed at your event, podcast, YouTube, conferences, church,

ShaRhonda D. Williams 190

+faith&qid=1702059330&s=books&sprefix=fa
mily+driven+%2Cstripbooks%2C138&sr=1-1

18. **Kingdom Woman by Tony Evans and daughter Chrystal Evans Hurst**

https://www.amazon.com/Kingdom-
Woman-Embracing-Purpose-
Possibilities/dp/1624053548/ref=sr_1_1?crid
=31CNWHMWD4XYW&keywords=kingdom+
woman&qid=1695236652&s=books&sprefix=k
ingdom+woman%2Cstripbooks%2C128&sr=1-1

19. **Kingdom Man by Tony Evans**

https://www.amazon.com/Kingdom-Man-
Every-Destiny-
Womans/dp/1589977475/ref=sr_1_1?crid=2M
7ZF95ALZ421&keywords=kingdom+man&qid
=1695236699&s=books&sprefix=kingdom+ma
n+%2Cstripbooks%2C121&sr=1-1

20. **Kingdom Marriage by Tony Evans**

https://www.amazon.com/Kingdom-
Marriage-Connecting-Purpose-
Pleasure/dp/1589978900/ref=sr_1_1_sspa?cri
d=2JQ1MILK2ZWBK&keywords=kingdom+m
arriage&qid=1695236770&s=books&sprefix=ki

ngdom+marriage%2Cstripbooks%2C143&sr=1-
1-
spons&sp_csd=d2lkZ2V0TmFtZT1zcF9hdGY&
psc=1

Sinners Prayer

"HAVE MERCY ON ME, O GOD, ACCORDING TO YOUR UNFAILING LOVE; ACCORDING TO YOUR GREAT COMPASSION BLOT OUT MY TRANSGRESSIONS. WASH AWAY ALL MY INIQUITY AND CLEANSE ME FROM MY SIN. FOR I KNOW MY TRANSGRESSIONS, AND MY SIN IS ALWAYS BEFORE ME. AGAINST YOU, YOU ONLY, HAVE I SINNED AND DONE WHAT IS EVIL IN YOUR SIGHT, SO THAT YOU ARE PROVED RIGHT WHEN YOU SPEAK AND JUSTIFIED WHEN YOU JUDGE. SURELY I HAVE BEEN A SINNER FROM BIRTH, SINFUL FROM THE TIME MY MOTHER CONCEIVED ME... CLEANSE ME WITH HYSSOP, AND I WILL BE CLEAN; WASH ME AND I WILL BE WHITER THAN SNOW... CREATE IN ME A PURE HEART, O GOD, AND RENEW A STEADFAST SPIRIT WITHIN ME. DO NOT CAST ME FROM YOUR PRESENCE OR TAKE YOUR HOLY SPIRIT FROM ME. RESTORE TO ME THE JOY OF YOUR SALVATION AND GRANT ME A WILLING SPIRIT TO SUSTAIN ME. THEN WILL I TEACH TRANSGRESSORS YOUR WAYS, AND SINNERS WILL TURN BACK TO YOU."

Psalm 51 NIV

ShaRhonda D. Williams188

Peace, in your mind, body, and soul

About The Author

ShaRhonda D. Williams is a beacon of hope and a testament to the transformative power of God's love and grace. As an author, speaker, and advocate for spiritual healing and restoration, ShaRhonda shares her journey of overcoming adversity with unwavering faith and resilience.

Born and raised in a tumultuous environment, ShaRhonda experienced firsthand the devastating effects of domestic violence, trauma, and sin. However, her life took a dramatic turn when she encountered the redeeming love of Jesus Christ. Through His grace, ShaRhonda found the strength to break free from the chains of her past and embrace a life of purpose and fulfillment.

ShaRhonda's writings reflect her deep-rooted commitment to spreading the message of hope, forgiveness, and spiritual renewal. Her candid memoirs and insightful teachings inspire others to confront their own struggles and seek healing through faith and repentance.

With a heart full of compassion and a desire to see lives transformed, ShaRhonda continues to share her story with audiences around the world. Through her books, speaking engagements, and online platforms, she empowers individuals to embrace the freedom and peace that can only be found in Christ.

ShaRhonda resides in the great state of Texas, where she enjoys spending time with her family, homeschooling, homemaking, blogging, and spreading the message of God's unfailing love.

Stay Connected:

Request to speak or be interviewed at your event, podcast, YouTube, conferences, church,

Peace, in your mind, body, and soul

domestic violence, school, or motherhood,
event may be sent to the email below:
Email: authorsharhonda@gmail.com
Join her email list to stay updated with the
latest releases.
Blog and more information:
www.sharhondadwilliams.com
Podcast: ShaRhonda, The Author
Youtube: ShaRhonda, The Author
Instagram: ShaRhonda, The Author
No other social medias at this time.

ShaRhonda D. Williams|191

Peace, in your mind, body, and soul

Release of the second edition

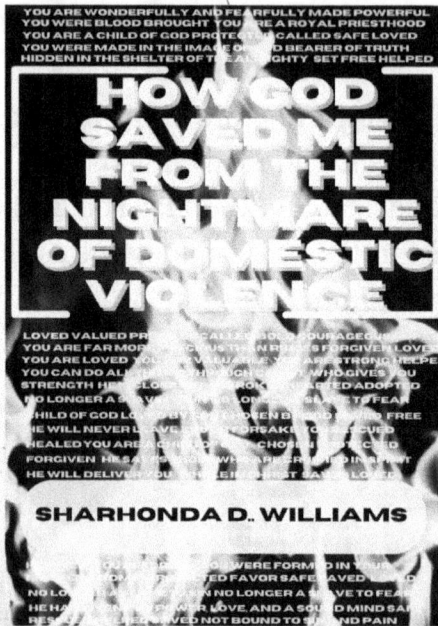

YOU ARE WONDERFULLY AND FEARFULLY MADE POWERFUL YOU WERE BLOOD BROUGHT YOU ARE A ROYAL PRIESTHOOD YOU ARE A CHILD OF GOD PROTECTED CALLED SAFE LOVED YOU WERE MADE IN THE IMAGE OF GOD BEARER OF TRUTH HIDDEN IN THE SHELTER OF THE ALMIGHTY SET FREE HELPED

HOW GOD SAVED ME FROM THE NIGHTMARE OF DOMESTIC VIOLENCE

SHARHONDA D. WILLIAMS

This is the second edition of my formerly named Battered & Broken The Nightmare Of Domestic Violence. The cautionary tale shows the readers how the author's desperation for love almost cost her life. It was a difficult battle she had to fight fiercely to escape the consequences of her poor choices. She received freedom by crying out to a holy God and she wants you to know that anyone else can recieve the same freedom if they ask for it. She breaks down the psychological things going on with her during this tulmultus relationship. She is bold, courageous, and fearless in her account how God saved her from the nightmare of domestic violenece.

Avaliable for purchase anywhere books are sold. More information on the book and the author can be found at www.sharhondadwilliams.com

SharRhonda D. Williams192

Peace, in your mind, body, and soul

Did God tell you to write a book?

WELCOME TO OUR SELF-PUBLISHING COMPANY, WHERE WE ARE DEDICATED TO EMPOWERING THOSE CALLED BY GOD TO SHARE THEIR STORIES WITH THE WORLD. WE BELIEVE THAT EACH WRITER HAS BEEN DIVINELY CHOSEN TO BE A VESSEL OF GOD'S TRUTH, SPREADING THEIR TESTIMONY LIKE ARROWS ACROSS THE GLOBE THROUGH THE MEDIUM OF BOOKS. AS IT IS WRITTEN, "AND THEY HAVE CONQUERED HIM BY THE BLOOD OF THE LAMB AND BY THE WORD OF THEIR TESTIMONY" (REVELATION 12:11). THE WORLD EAGERLY AWAITS YOUR TESTIMONY, AND THROUGH WRITING, YOUR VOICE CANNOT BE SILENCED. DON'T HESITATE ANY LONGER—TAKE THE NEXT STEP IN FULFILLING YOUR DIVINE PURPOSE TODAY.
"THEY OVERCOME BY THE BLOOD OF THE LAMB, AND THE WORD OF THEIR TESTIMONY." REVELATIONS 12:11

IF YOU SENSE THE LEADING OF THE HOLY SPIRIT, WE INVITE YOU TO REACH OUT TO US AT WWW.CHOSENBYGODPUBLISHING.COM.
AT OUR SELF-PUBLISHING COMPANY, ALL RIGHTS TO YOUR BOOK REMAIN YOURS TO KEEP. HOWEVER, TO BRING YOUR BOOK TO LIFE, YOU MUST MAKE AN INITIAL INVESTMENT. THROUGH YOUR OBEDIENCE TO GOD'S CALLING, YOU'LL REAP THE BENEFITS OF YOUR BOOK FOR A LIFETIME. TAKE THE FIRST STEP TOWARD SHARING YOUR MESSAGE WITH THE WORLD TODAY.

ShaRhonda D. Williams193